INCREASE
YOUR
INSURANCE

SALES, RETENTION & REFERRALS

NOW!!!

By Melvin Pierre, Sr.

Proven Systems, Activities & Processes To Help <u>YOU</u> Increase Your <u>Sales,</u> <u>Retention, & Referrals</u>

authorHOUSE®

AuthorHouse™
1663 Liberty Drive, Suite 200
Bloomington, IN 47403
www.authorhouse.com
Phone: 1-800-839-8640

First published by AuthorHouse 3/9/2009

ISBN: 978-1-4389-4774-7 (sc)

Printed in the United States of America
Bloomington, Indiana

This book is printed on acid-free paper.

Acknowledgments

After watching me prepare and deliver training sessions and motivational speeches in various settings all over the country, my wife has urged me, for years, to assemble the "best" of those sessions in a book.....and, for years, I promised her that I would do just that. But then.... one day in September, 2007, it's like I was "touched by another angel with a "<u>message</u>" who simply said "Pierre.... you need to write a book about your experiences in this business!" And that's the day that I actually made the commitment to both of them that I would indeed write this book. Fifty-Six (56) weekends later, it became a reality.

<u>July 24, 2008</u> marked my 30th year in the Insurance Industry......22 years as an <u>Agent</u>....and 8 years in <u>Sales Management.</u> And what a rewarding career it has been!!! My journey down this career path was started at my kitchen table. I was in the process of switching my Homeowners Policy from an agent that I had never met...seen or heard from. Instead of giving me a "fast quote" over the phone, my "new" Agent, <u>Richard Kelt, Sr.,</u> made an "appointment" to come out to the house....where he had an opportunity to review the current policy.... explain the coverages.....offer several options to upgrade the policy......and was so "passionate" about this policy and his career that we starting talking about career opportunities (for me) with his company. At the end of his "consultation" on Homeowners Insurance, he stated

1

that, in <u>HIS</u> opinion, I would be a "good candidate" for the insurance business. At that point in my life, I was the Assistant Administrator of The Bureau of Food Stamps in the Department of Finance for the City of New Orleans. I had no sales experience whatsoever......but <u>HE</u> thought that I would be a "good candidate!" And he didn't just "talk the talk,".......he "walked the walk"...took it to the next level.... and made an "appointment" for me to be interviewed by one of the District Sales Managers, Mr. Linden Bethune. And here we are....30 YEARS LATER!!!! I was simply looking to buy a <u>Homeowners Policy</u>.....and was offered a <u>CAREER</u>. Richard & Lin, <u>Thank You</u> for your vision, encouragement and your support!!! That single event....at my kitchen table....on Petit Bayou Lane in New Orleans.......changed the entire course of my life.

As we travel down the "Highway of Life," it's amazing how <u>"SPECIAL PEOPLE"</u> and <u>"SPECIAL EVENTS"</u> are, strategically, placed in our lives......at certain mile markers, exits, rest stops, detours, traffic-jams, cross-roads and bumps in the road.... to help lead us to our destiny. To all of the <u>"SPECIAL PEOPLE"</u> who have "touched my life" in any way, I want to say <u>THANK YOU</u> and I dedicate this book to YOU!!!!

The Purpose of This Book

As I stated before, when I entered the Insurance Industry in 1978, I had no sales experience whatsoever! Fortunately, I had the opportunity to surround myself with some of the ***Top Producers of Life, Auto, Home, Flood and Commercial Insurance.*** They all had one thing in common: "Systems, Activities and Processes" to achieve their goals. They achieved their goals "on purpose" and not "by accident." They started each year.... with the END RESULTS in mind and in focus. They all had a very definite "Road Map to Success."

Looking back on three decades in this business, my goal here is to share a few of the most effective and productive

"Agent-Level Marketing Systems, Activities and Processes" that I have:

*   Observed Other Agents Successfully Executing.
*   Personally Installed & Implemented As An Agent In "Real Life" Settings During Consultations.
*   Taught Others To Use As A Field Sales Manager over a 30 year period. I can GUARANTEE you, in advance, that nothing in this book will be complicated or hard to understand. We invite YOU to "Follow The Tracks" step-by-step.

My hope is that you will implement those *systems,* *activities and processes* that fit "your style" and "your way" of doing business and that <u>YOU</u> will become one of the "movers and shakers" and "major playmakers" in your organization.

In this book, I want to share four (4) "<u>Agent-Level</u>" Systems that I've used for three (3) decades. They are as follows:

1. An Easy-To-Install "<u>Life Marketing System</u>" that I call "<u>Life Made Easy</u>" ....that was developed as a result of working side-by-side with two of the Top Life Producers in the company. This system helped me to join <u>THEM</u> as one of the Top Life Insurance Producers in the company as well. As a Sales Manager, I've shared this system with agents in my assigned markets and several of them have also become very Successful Life Insurance Producers.

2. During my first Presidents Conference, one of the guest speakers was an agent who had built a $10,000,000 per year operation and the "secret to his success" was to "<u>Succeed On A DAILY BASIS</u>." As an agent, I was able to incorporate virtually all of his activities and processes into a system that I call the <u>2/10/1 Production Plan.</u> As a Territory Sales Manager, I shared this system with the agents in my assigned market and moved an entire market from "last to first" in Auto & Homeowners Production. One of the agents in that particular market became the "Rookie of The Year!" To this

day, I consider her to be one of my best "students" ever. She was willing to <u>"listen, learn and execute."</u> I challenge YOU to do the same.

3. I also want to share the concept of "<u>Full-Circle Selling"</u> with you....where the goal is to concentrate on installing the "Basic Three Lines"- <u>Auto, Home & Life</u> in EACH of your households... in an effort to "insulate" your clients from the competition. When you have a situation where there is more than one agent in a household, there are "<u>Too many Chefs in the kitchen!!!</u>" As you already know, <u>MULTI-LINING</u> is one of the main "keys" to increasing your <u>RETENTION</u>.

4. For years, we've "partnered" with our clients and prospects and worked a "Geometric Progression" and/or Multi-Level Marketing Referral System to create an <u>UNLIMITED</u> source of <u>REFERRALS.</u>

We'll discuss each of the above systems in detail....and, if you decide to install these systems in your agency, you'll be on your way to <u>INCREASING YOUR INSURANCE SALES, RETENTION & REFERRALS.</u>

MP

Table of Contents

The Policy That Can Insure

The Family's Income!

Without a doubt, if you are working with a company that offers Life Insurance....... in my opinion, Life Insurance is one of the <u>most important policies</u> that you have to offer to clients and prospects. It's the policy that can insure the "<u>C</u>hief <u>E</u>xecutive <u>O</u>fficer(s)" of the family and, thus, the family's income! It's the policy that can be designed to (1) pay off the mortgage and keep the home in the family, (2) send the kids to college, (3) pay off all of the bills for the family, (4) provide a monthly income for the family as well as (5) pay final expenses.....in the event of the premature death of the financial provider(s). It's amazing to me how many clients demand <u>FULL REPLACEMENT COST PROTECTION</u> on their homes and personal property.......and <u>FULL REPLACEMENT COST PROTECTION</u> on their cars, boats, motorcycles, and the other "material things," but have to "think about" insuring the <u>CEO</u> of the family for <u>FULL REPLACEMENT VALUE.</u> It's amazing how people are willing to pay $500 per month car notes (on a depreciating asset), $200 per month on Auto Insurance, $150 per month for the Digital Phone-Internet & Cable TV package ...but have to <u>"think about"</u> setting aside $150 per month to insure the <u>"income"</u> of the "CEO" of the family (many of whom are making over $100,000 per year and could generate over $1,000,000 of income for the family in a ten year period and well over

$2,000,000 of "family income" in a twenty year period. It's all about choices and priorities. It's also about how we, as agents, feel about the "opportunity to serve others" and how we "position" the conversation. I can do an entire presentation on "life insurance" without ever using the words "life insurance." Many clients and prospects are not interested in talking about "life insurance".....but they are <u>VERY INTERESTED</u> in discussing ways to protect the "financial future" of their loved ones. Instead of selling "Life Insurance," <u>subliminally</u> I'm selling MONEY FOR THEIR FAMILY'S FUTURE! Same concept.....Different approach. If a prospect is earning $80,000 per year......I can demonstrate in very easy-to-understand language how they can buy ten (10) years of income($800,000)..... twenty (20) years of income ($1,600,000) or even thirty (30) years of income ($2,400,000)....RIGHT NOW....IN ADVANCE!!! If they qualify physically and are willing to pay the monthly premium, we can help them to create an INSTANT ESTATE. On the day that they <u>STEP OUT</u>........ the INSURANCE COMPANY will <u>STEP IN</u> with the CASH to take care of their family. That's just one of the ways to "insure the family's income" and protect the "financial future" of their loved. WOW!!!!! What a concept! What an opportunity!

<u>Several Industry Surveys</u> <u>Show The Following:</u>

- That the "Family's Income" in millions of households across North America is NOT INSURED ....because "millions of families" have NO LIFE INSURANCE at all.

- Many other families are woefully <u>UNDERINSURED</u>.

- There are others who are depending on the GROUP LIFE INSURANCE at a job that they may not have 60 days or even 60 minutes from now.

- The bottom line is that many families are simply NOT FINANCIALLY PREPARED for the premature death of the financial provider(s) of the family.

WHY?

We, As An Industry, And As Agents, **HAVE** What They Need!

. . . .

So Why Don't **THEY HAVE** What They Need?

. . . .

Have We Offered Them An "**Opportunity**" To Get What They Need?

That Is The Question!!!

So Here's An Opportunity For ALL OF US

To Make A Difference

In The Lives Of Others!

This Is Your Call To Action!!!

I am, personally, calling on **each and every *Agent* and each and every *Life Insurance Company*** in NORTH AMERICA that has the "ability and the facilities" to offer LIFE INSURANCE......to reach out to EVERY ONE OF YOUR CURRENT CLIENTS and ALL of your "past, present and future prospects" and offer them the following:

1. A "Complimentary, No-Obligation, No Strings Attached, Easy To Access and Easy To Understand......Needs Analysis."

2. An Explanation of The Available Features, Benefits and Options to Insure the "Financial Future" of their family.

3. A "Free Review" Each and Every Year.

I would <u>ASK</u> you....and <u>CHALLENGE</u> you to "<u>TAKE THE LEAD</u>" ...and become a driving force.......in a "<u>Life Across America Campaign</u>,".... and/or a "<u>Life Across Canada Campaign</u>"....and/or "<u>The Life Across North America Campaign.</u>"

"*LIFE ACROSS AMERICA CAMPAIGN*"

Where There's <u>LIFE</u>.....

There's <u>HOPE</u> For A Brighter Tomorrow!!!

"*LIFE ACROSS CANADA CAMPAIGN*"

Because Where There's <u>LIFE</u>.....

There's <u>A Future</u> For Generations To Come!

"LIFE ACROSS NORTH AMERICA CAMPAIGN"

Because Where There's <u>LIFE</u>.....

There's <u>HOPE</u> For Generations To Come!

Whatever name you choose to call this initiative....we've got lots of work to do! And it's going to take ***ALL OF US...All Across North America***...to offer the millions of American & Canadian families... who don't have any Life Insurance or enough Life Insurance......... the "opportunity" to ***"insure and secure"*** the financial future of their family. I'm of the opinion that <u>each generation</u> should be "better off financially" than the previous one...and the proceeds from Life Insurance is one of the financial vehicles that can be used to help accomplish that goal. It makes no sense to me for a family to still be in a position where they are "struggling financially" after 2 and 3 generations have already passed this way. The position that <u>WE</u> are in....as Professional Agents...is so powerful that we can literally "<u>CHANGE TOMORROW</u>" with an application <u>TODAY</u>. I ACCEPT THAT RESPONSIBILITY!! What about <u>YOU</u>?

What WE Know
That Our Clients & Prospects
NEED TO KNOW

We know that.....if a prospect or a client is making $100,000 per year.....and should pass away prematurely, not only is there the devastating lost of a loved one... but....the family would also **_suffer a loss of income_** of $1,000,000 in a 10 year period......$2,000,000 in a 20 year period.....and $3,000,000 in a 30 year period. We have no way to replace the human being.......but we, as Insurance Professionals, have been trained......and are in a position to help them put **_"affordable plans in place"_** to "insure and protect" the **_income_** for that family......... so that they will have the "options and the opportunity" to continue on the same standard of living to which they've become accustomed... as they travel down the "Highway of Life."

YOU

CAN

MAKE A DIFFERENCE!

What Our Clients & Prospects NEED TO KNOW & UNDERSTAND

In the event of the premature death of the financial provider(s) or "CEO" of the family, they <u>NEED TO KNOW</u> the answers to the questions below:

- How much the family would need to pay off the mortgage or, in the case of a renter, how much the family would need to just pay cash for a home and stop having to rent.   _____

- How much the family would need to send their kid(s) to college?   _____

- How much the family would need <u>monthly</u> to continue living on their same standard of living?   _____

- How much the family would need to pay off all of the bills?   _____

- How much the family would need for final expenses
      _____

- <u>Total Amount Of CASH Needed:</u>   _____

- Total Amount <u>Currently Available</u>:   _____

- <u>Additional Amount</u> Needed To Protect The Family
      _____

Keep it simple......

Ask the questions in that exact order. Speak from **_"Your Heart to Their Heart."_** Let the clients and prospects tell <u>YOU</u> what **THEIR FAMILY NEEDS ARE!!** Offer them two (2) or three (3) solutions to solve <u>THEIR PROBLEM.</u> After offering the solutions.....ask one final question: **_"Which one do you feel more comfortable with?"_** When they answer that final question, start writing the application.

DO THEY REALLY KNOW????

How many of your clients and prospects have ever been offered the opportunity "to qualify...... to reserve" a $1,000,000 policy for their loved ones for a 10-20- or 30 year period? And the reason that I'm using the term "reserve" is because that $1,000,000 will be "on reserve" for their loved ones "permanently"(if they select a permanent plan) or it will be "on reserve" for the "term" that they select......hopefully, with the option to convert it to a permanent plan.

Are your clients and prospects (age 40 and under) aware of the fact that, in many cases, a $1,000,000 term policy can be obtained for less than $100 per month (based on their age, health, and the other underwriting requirements)? From MY perspective, I'm offering clients and prospects the opportunity to "purchase" $1,000,000 (or whatever the face amount of the policy may be) for $100.00 per month (or whatever the monthly premium may be). When I make a presentation to a client or prospect, I very seldom use the words "Life Insurance" because I don't know what those words means to THEM! I offer them an opportunity to "set aside" the exact amount of CASH that they want to PASS ON to their loved ones. Whatever amount that THEY choose... has a MONTHLY PREMIUM involved to keep THEIR money "on reserve" for THEIR FAMILY. They understand THAT EXPLANATION (and most of the objections fade away because we keep the focus on "Insuring & Securing" the "Financing Future" Of THEIR Loved Ones).

How many of your clients and prospects know that they can "start" off with a $1,000,000......10....20 or 30 year term policy.....and then exercise the "option to convert" it to a permanent plan at a later date? So why order a paramed exam and have them go through underwriting and all of that for $250,000.....when they can go through underwriting ONCE IN A LIFETIME (at age 25, 30, 35 or 40).......and, perhaps, qualify for $1,000,000 or more....and then have COMPLETE CONTROL over the "option to convert" it. As you and your clients move forward, hopefully, you'll have the type of policy where "partial"conversions are allowed. This will put your client in a position to convert ½ (or whatever amount is desired) to a permanent plan.... while keeping the other ½ (or whatever amount remains) AS IT IS..... until the term expires. At any rate, once that $1,000,000 policy is issued, you've, at least, GUARANTEED that family $1,000,000 of protection........and now THEY have complete control over that $1,000,000 BLOCK OF PROTECTION....without any further evidence of insurability in most cases.

<u>MILLIONS</u>

<u>OF</u>

<u>FAMILIES</u>

<u>Need Us NOW........More Than Ever!!!</u>

<u>Opportunity Is Knocking</u>

And

<u>Immediate</u>
<u>Action</u>
<u>Is</u>
<u>Required</u>

Let's _**REFRESH & RESET**_ The Market Place

We Need **ALL HANDS ON DECK** Now!!!

- There are many families who still have a _**Decreasing Term**_ policy and don't realize that the premium is <u>level</u> but the <u>coverage is decreasing</u>!!! And may not have seen <u>that</u> agent since they bought the policy.

- There are many families who only have _**Accidental Death Policies**_ and are under the impression that they will receive payment for a natural death. <u>WE</u> know that's not true.....but they don't!!

- There are many families who have a $25,000 Graded Death policy and are under the impression that they will receive payment for $25,000 immediately...upon the death of a loved one.... without realizing that the policy must be in effect for XXXX number of years before it will pay the face amount. <u>WE</u> know....but they don't. And that may be one of the reasons that a medical exam or the answers to medical questions were not required at the time of application.

- There are many families who were "pressured and encouraged" to cash in policies, that had already _**survived and surpassed**_ the "Contestability Period," in exchange for other policies that would be of more benefit to the <u>agent</u> than the client.

- Then, there are those who may have bought the old door-to-door "debit" policies (like my family did when I was young)...... who will be in for the "surprise of their life" should a love one pass away.

- There are many companies that are still willing to offer a 50 year old male or female... a 30 year term policy with _**level premiums**_ and a _**level face amount**_ Our clients and prospects, in that age bracket <u>NEED</u> <u>TO KNOW</u> that....because that policy could run from age 50 to age 80 with the same face amount and same premium.....and provide many families "security" and "peace of mind" for 30 years. That's an "awesome" marketing opportunity all by itself!!

- If you represent a company that offers the new _**"Return of Premiums Term Policies,"**_ you may have an advantage in the market place and your clients and prospects **NEED TO KNOW** about those options as well.

- If you ask clients and prospects WHY they bought a $50,000 whole life policy or a $100,000 Term Policy, or a $250,000 Universal Life Policy, in many cases, they can't tell you WHY. In many cases, they bought it because that's what the "agent" wanted to sell that day...week....or month.

- If you ask them how they arrived at ANY amount, in many cases, they can't tell you WHY....... because, unfortunately, many "agents" won't take the time to offer a "free-needs analysis" to help them determine how much is <u>really</u> needed. In many cases, they just bought what the "agent" was pushing that day...that week or that month to meet their sales quotas....and many of those "policy pushers" are no longer in the business to see the damage that <u>has been done</u> or <u>will be done</u> as a result of their actions.

<u>Let's Make It Right!!</u>

- If you should offer your clients a Term Life Insurance Policy, please do not offer a one year or a five year renewable term to solve a 20 year problem. <u>THEY</u> may not know the difference..... but <u>WE DO!</u>

- If you should offer your clients a Term Life Insurance Policy, please offer a 10, 20 or 30 year plan where the <u>Premium </u>stays the same and the <u>Face Amount</u> stays the same for the entire period (and states it in the contract).....and please give them the <u>"opportunity"</u> to convert those policies to permanent policies by reviewing those policies with them on an Annual Basis.

- Please do not offer any more Decreasing Term Policies. Clients may not know the difference.... but WE DO!

- If you offer your clients a Universal Life Policy, please take the time to explain all of the features and benefits and fund the policy properly.

- Please make an appointment with each and every one of your current clients and LET THEM TALK to you about what THEIR loved ones would need in the event of the premature passing of the family's "financial provider(s)." Many of them have NEVER been offered the opportunity to have a "Complimentary" needs analysis done for them. Many have never SEEN a needs-analysis. Show them a "sample" of one and prepare one for them. EVERY FAMILY needs to know the answers to the questions whether they buy or not.

- Consider the following "sample" needs-analysis:

How Much _CASH_ Would YOUR FAMILY NEED TO:

1. To pay off the mortgage $195,000
2. Send YOUR Kids To College $200,000
3. Provide $3,000 Per Month for 10 Years to Your Family
                                                             $360,000
4. To pay off all the bills??? $ 46,000
5. Final Expenses $ 25,000

Summary:

Total **CASH** Needed:	**$826,000**
Currently Available:	**$250,000**
Additional **CASH** Needed:	**$576,000**

- Notice the "absence" of the words "Life Insurance" in the above example. The "needs-analysis" should be the "centerpiece" of the consultation. It gives clients the opportunity to "see the big picture" as opposed to just a $50,000 or $100,000 need. Unfortunately, many people have NEVER had a needs-analysis done for them. We owe them that much...whether they buy or not.

- So "paint the entire picture" for them and then show two (2) or three (3) options to "insure and secure" the financial future of their family. Don't try to "count their dollars" in advance. Some agents like to ask the question: ***"How Much Can You Afford To Set Aside To Protect Your Family's Future?"*** Prepare the "solutions"......explain the features and benefits of each solution (to THEIR PROBLEM) and let them choose the one that they are "more comfortable with." Don't "insult" their intelligence by asking them "How much can you afford?" After all, we're talking about securing the FINANCIAL FUTURE of THEIR family. Many people are paying $150 per month to the cable company for the "cable T.V., internet and phone service package," so why should I be "afraid" or "reluctant" to let them know that it will ***only*** cost them $99 per month or $139 per month for a $1,000,000 policy to "insure and secure" the FINANCIAL FUTURE of <u>THEIR</u> family.

- By the way....just so they know...... there is no **_CASH VALUE_** or **_RETURN OF PREMIUMS_** or **_RETURN OF PAYMENTS_** from the investment in the "Cable TV" package. Some clients and prospects try to use the "what's the cash value" excuse or objection at times. As you know, the policies that develop the highest "cash values," in most cases, will have the highest monthly premium as well.... so then you'll get the "cost too much" excuse or objection. We'll show you how to overcome that too. At the end of the day, here's what I can tell you....from experience. As an agent, we have a duty and an obligation to offer our clients an "opportunity" to protect the "financial future" of **_THEIR FAMILY_**. Some folks <u>will be</u> receptive... and some folks <u>won't be</u> receptive...but once we've given them that opportunity, we've placed the "ball" in their court. Isn't it amazing how many excuses people can come up with....not realizing that we're talking to them about protecting **_THEIR FAMILY'S FINANCIAL FUTURE!!!_** We're talking to them about putting a "contract in place" whereby on the day that "they step out" our company will "step in!!!" Sometimes, you have to literally sell them on protecting their OWN FAMILY. And remember this....IF AND WHEN they say <u>NO</u>.... they're not saying <u>NO</u> to you. They're saying <u>NO</u> to their OWN FAMILY. So don't get discouraged. And don't take it personally. We've got work to do! Keep doing **_YOUR PART_**. That's the only part that

27

you can control and be responsible for....**_YOUR PART!_**

- At some point in time, you will have to deliver a policy that has been "rated" due to the Medical History or Current Medical Condition of a client. If you find yourself in that position, here's a suggestion: When you call for the appointment to deliver the policy, let them know that you've got GREAT NEWS..... "the application has been APPROVED." Bring a copy of their needs-analysis and the new policy and let them know that, based on THEIR Medical History or a Current Medical Condition, the application was approved as follows:

  1.
  2.
  3.

  and then discuss the terms and conditions of the underwriting offer. It is....what it is. They are.... Who they are. Their age is THEIR AGE. They are a smoker or a non-smoker. They are in "good health" or they're not in "good health." Their Cholesterol levels may be up or down.....good or bad. They have "high blood pressure" or they don't have "high blood pressure." If they do....they do....and the policy will be rated accordingly. But it's not YOUR FAULT!! It is...what it is.....whatever it is!! I've seen agents get upset with the underwriters as a result of the policy being rated. In my opinion, that's not proper or professional.

Human Nature

I don't know about your clients.....but I'll tell you what I found out about my clients and about "human nature" in general.

- Most folks like to talk about <u>THEMSELVES</u>.... and <u>THEIR FAMILY MEMBERS</u>. (So I like to talk about <u>Them</u> and <u>Their Family Members</u> as well.)

- Most folks like to have things <u>THEIR WAY</u>. (So I make sure that they have things <u>Their Way</u>... because......if a client can't do business the way that they want to do business....why should they do business with you at all?) Today....they want to have the option to call, click or visit. <u>LISTEN</u> very carefully to what they're <u>SAYING</u>....and also to what they are <u>NOT SAYING</u>...and "play the music" in the <u>KEY</u> that they want the music played in! That's "music to their ears."

- Most folks want to know what's in it for <u>ME, ME, ME & ME?</u> (So I talk about what's in it for <u>Them, Them, Them</u> and <u>Them</u>!)

- They want to know "What can you do for <u>ME, ME, ME & ME</u>?" (So I "Show & Tell" them what our Products and Services can do for Them, Them, Them, and Them...because... if that connection is not made, <u>There Will Be No Sale</u>!)

- When they want SERVICE, they want SERVICE NOW! (When <u>WE</u> want Service, <u>WE</u> want Service NOW...and our Clients are no different from us.)

That being said, my entire "consultation" is centered around them..... their family members......what's in it for them and what we can do for them. When you can "address" those points....... as you move through the "consultation," you can eliminate many objections....... IN ADVANCE.

<u>Two Very Successful Closing Techniques</u>

Let's take a look at "<u>The BLANK CHECK CLOSE</u>"......and "<u>The MILLION DOLLAR BILL CLOSE</u>." The focus is clearly on THEM.....THEIR FAMILY MEMBERS......what's in it for THEM and what we can do for THEM. It's ALL about THEM! And it's hard for THEM to walk away from this issue now. At this point in the consultation, they have had a "major revelation".............they know that THEIR FAMILY MEMBERS would be in serious financial trouble if they fail to take action NOW. The only discussion now is HOW MUCH COVERAGE they want to put in place TODAY. So it's time to get serious and CLOSE THE SALE.

- **The _BLANK CHECK_ Close:**

Take a company produced envelope.....with the company logo on it.....and make it look like a "Blank Check" as follows:

Company Logo Here   Date:_____ Pay to the order of_____\$_____ _____Dollars For_____   _____

After completing the needs-analysis (and whatever you do, don't under-estimate the power of the needs-analysis).......and after you've offered the solutions, there may be a need for $576,000 or $825,000 or a $1,000,000 or more......and your client may be "reluctant" to make a decision and move forward with that particular amount. So put the pen in the hand of the client and ask them to make the check out for the "amount" that they feel comfortable with.........and make it payable to the "person or persons" of their choice. Once they've completed the check.....start writing the application.

- **The _MILLION DOLLAR BILL_ Close:**

I have two laminated "Million Dollar Bills" that I've used for years to close Life Sales. There is a company that makes "Million Dollar Bills" as a novelty. I've never seen an actual Million Dollar bill and I would venture to say that most of my clients haven't seen one either. But these "Million Dollar Bills" can set the stage and provide a great visual effect. I have personally used them to close several Million Dollar Sales as follows:

If there is a "need" for a $1,000,000 policy......and I sense "reluctance" on the part of the client, I'll place my $1,000,000 dollar bill on the table and make the following statement:

"If you are willing to "set aside" $100 per month.....$150 per month (or whatever the monthly premium may be in that particular case), we are willing to "set aside" $1,000,000 for YOUR FAMILY. If you'll do your part, we'll do our part. And on the day that you "step out," we'll "step in" with the money to take care of your family. Is that important to you?" If the answer is YES, start writing the application.

Reach Out And Touch _EVERY ONE_ Of Your Clients

If we can encourage you to reach out to EVERY ONE OF YOUR CURRENT CLIENTS and put a policy in place that, ultimately, protects the financial future of just ONE family in the event of the premature death of the "financial provider," (I'm talking about just ONE FAMILY who didn't have the proper coverage prior to YOU contacting them)........then this entire effort would have been worth it.

Build The Foundation Of The Financial Pyramid First!

Let's talk about the "Financial Pyramid." Some agents try to build it from the top down...with Stocks, Bonds, Mutual Funds, and other investment products (because that may be THEIR SPECIALTY and that's what they want to promote)........... but neglect to "insure and protect" the family's INCOME ...which is the basic source of all of the money to do all of those other things. When you consider the fact that MILLIONS OF FAMILIES have no Life Insurance at all, that tells me that there's a need for us to "circle back" and help those families to build a firm foundation FIRST. All we're asking you to do is to help your clients to complete **STEP ONE:** The "Foundation"............. with Basic Life Insurance Solutions. Put a policy in place to protect the family's INCOME....and go back every year thereafter and add other products to the portfolio as needed. When I started talking to clients and prospects....in plain Engish....and plain terms.... about insuring the "FAMILY'S INCOME, that seemed like a "new concept" to them and my sales took "off like a rocket"........with little or no resistance.

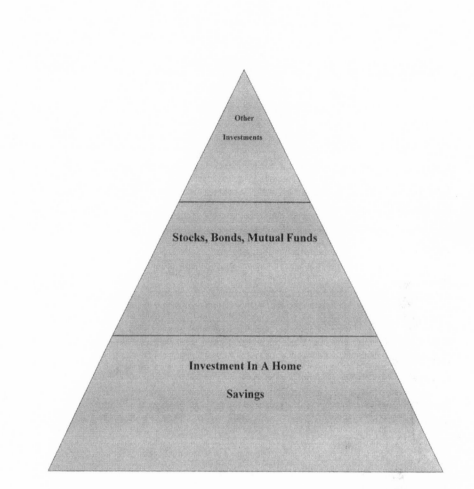

Other Investments

Stocks, Bonds, Mutual Funds

Investment In A Home

Savings

<u>INSURE THE FAMILY'S INCOME FIRST</u>

<u>Step One (1) An INSTANT ESTATE</u>...........
<u>LIFE INSURANCE</u>

Create An Instant Estate.

Insure and Secure The "Income" & "Future Earnings" For The Family NOW!

Case Studies

Let's take a look into two households where the needs were basically the same in the year <u>2000</u>. Each family had a $200,000 Mortgage Balance.....2 young children, ages 2 & 5 and $25,000 of outstanding debt. Each financial provider... in each household... was a 30 year old male.....married to a 30 year old female. Both of the spouses were homemakers. The Annual Income in both families was $80,000. Family A had "Agent A" and Family B had "Agent B."

<u>Agent A</u> offered a complimentary "needs-analysis" and uncovered the following needs:

- Pay off the mortgage **$200,000**
- Education Fund For The Children **$200.000**
- Amount Needed To Provide $3,000 Per Month for 20 years **$720,000**
- Amount Needed To Pay Off Outstanding Debt

  $ 25,000
- Final Expenses **$ 15,000**

Total CASH Needed In The Event of Premature Death

$1,160,000

Current Coverage was Group Insurance at work

2 x $80,000 **$160,000**

Additional Coverage Needed **$1,000,000**

Family A understood the need to insure his "future earnings"...... the $80,000 per year. Agent A made it very clear that without him and the FAMILY'S INCOME, his family would be facing "financial disaster." After having the opportunity to review several options with their agent, they chose a 30 Year Term Policy with a CONVERSION OPTION. Six months later, he purchased a policy on his wife to add to their portfolio. One year later, during the Annual Review, he purchased a "College Plan" for each of his children. In 2007, he passed away and his family received the proceeds from the $1,000,000 Policy plus the $160,000 from the group insurance policy. Family A had all of the money that they needed to do all of the things that needed to be done!

Agent B did not take the time to complete a needs analysis for Family B because he was more interested in making a sale (any kind of sale) to meet HIS quota for that particular week. Agent B was very excited about the "New Whole Life Series" that his company was promoting. So he sold them a $100,000 Whole Life Policy....with all of the great new features and benefits, guaranteed Cash Values, Paid Up at 65, etc. But he never talked to the family about insuring the "Family's Income." Without the "Family's Income," everything STOPS. In 2007, the financial provider in Family B passed away as well. And this family received the proceeds from the $100,000 Life Policy. Just like Family A, there was a NEED for over $1,000,000.....but that need was not uncovered by Agent B. So, Family B is facing FINANCIAL DISASTER! Agent B wrote one policy for this family..... never came back to review the family's situation.....and is no longer in the business. Agent B didn't realize that he could have "started" the family's portfolio with a $1,000,000 Term

Policy (to insure the Family's Income first) and then convert $100,000 of that Term Policy into a Permanent Plan and this family would have received $1,000,000 as well. He has no idea what <u>Family B</u> is going through right now as a direct result of his actions.

Show Your Clients and Prospects How To:

- Provide Funds To Pay Off The Mortgage or Pay Cash For A New Home (if they are renters).
- Provide A College Education Fund For Their Children.
- Provide Funds That Will Guarantee A Monthly Income For The Family.
- Provide An Emergency Fund.
- Provide Funds To Pay Final Expenses.
- Provide Funds To Pay Off All Medical Bills.
- Provide Funds To Pay Off All Creditors.

Build The Foundation FIRST!

Add To The Portfolio LATER!

(It's O.K. to have a Term Policy, a UL and/or a Whole Life Policy in the portfolio to accomplish different objectives)

SYMPATHY IS NICE.......

But Your Clients Need A Check!!!

People often ask me:

Why Are You So **Passionate** About Life Insurance???

My First Encounter With Insurance Went Exactly Like This:

You Have My Deepest Sympathy!!!

When I was 10 years old, I remember having to open the door about 10 to 15 times a week for people who called themselves "insurance agents." They came to our house....each and every week.....to collect money on the "policies???" that they had "sold???" to my grandmother for insurance on my mother, myself, my grandmother and all of her other children like my uncles, aunts....... and all of their kids, distant cousins, and all of their cousins on both sides of the family. They always seemed to know when my grandmother had "their" money. They drank coffee with my grandmother and "pretended" to care about our family.......but....for some reason, it just didn't feel right to ME. All I know is that my grandmother had four (4) children of her own........ a 6th grade education................ And shoe boxes full of "so-called" insurance policies....and it seemed to me like she was working to pay on all of these policies each week!!

Then......the "unexpected" happened on July 29, 1964. My 31 year old mother had the opportunity to have breakfast......and lunch that day.....but no dinner. At 3:30pm., on July 29, 1964........ which started out to be a beautiful summer day, my 31 year old mother experienced "numbness on the left side of her body" and was rushed to an emergency room in downtown New Orleans where she had a heart attack and died..... while sitting and waiting.....and sitting and waiting.... and sitting and waiting for the "attending physicians" to attend to her and her condition. And here we are..... 44 years later....... And I still cannot find the words to describe how I felt going to that hospital and finding my mother "covered up" with a white sheet. One of the things that I learned that day is that "nobody....no matter how young or old...has a lease on life!" We may all look good on the "outside"....but who knows what we look like on the "inside!" I understood that.....on that day!!!

- As an "insurance consultant," one of the things that I always want my clients to fully be aware of is the sense of urgency in making "plans and preparations" to protect the "financial future" of their family!
- Many of us make great plans about what we're going to do and what we want to do when we reach the age of 65...without giving much consideration to the fact that we may not be HERE in the next 65 seconds!!

At any rate, at the end of that terrible day in July, when my grandmother and I got back home, we retrieved boxes of "policies" and pulled out all of the policies that had been "SOLD???" on the life of Rose Mae Pierre, my 31 year old mother. We were completely shocked to discover that all we had were policies with a Face Value of $300....$500.....$1,000.....and a "Burial Policy" that covered the cost of embalming, a hearse and two "limousines." <u>Total Insurance: $2,934!!!!</u> That's how my mother was buried. With a Burial Insurance Policy!!! Not only was she my mom...but she was the sole "financial provider" for the two of us. So how would "Little Melvin" (I was "Little Melvin" at that time) get from Age 16 to Age 18....and then go on to college? And what did all of those "policy pushers" have to offer "Little Melvin?

<u>Here's The Exact Quote</u>

<u>"You Have My Deepest Sympathy!!! If There's Anything That I Can Do, Please Let Me Know."</u>

My mom was a gospel singer....so I heard those words.... at least...500 times from 500 different people (but no check was forthcoming!)

To the "Policy Pushers," who came to our door each and every week like clock-work, I'd like the answers to these questions:

What about the kid (ME) who opened the door each week for all of those "so-called" Insurance Premium Collectors??? What about <u>MY</u> future.....now that my mother (and my financial provider) was no longer there??? What was I suppose to do? I was on my way to the

10th grade. How was I suppose to get from age 16.........
through high school.................... and then on to college?
Where would the money come from for that? In the final
analysis, when it was all said and done.....none of these
"insurance premium collectors" had ever sat down with
my grandmother or my mother, with <u>OUR INTEREST AT
HEART,</u> and talked about helping any of them to insure
the "financial future" of <u>OUR</u> family (in the event of a
premature death). A premature death......my mother's
death.....had become a reality!!! NOW WHAT???

I remember all of these "insurance premium collectors"
coming over to the house to express their deepest
sympathy. And saying "If there's anything that <u>we</u> can
do.....please let us know." What could they do now? What
would they do...... if we had asked? Absolutely <u>NOTHING!</u>
What they should have done.....they didn't do!!
I'm still upset about it 44 years LATER!!!

I don't ever recall any of those "Policy Pushers" coming
over to the house and doing a "needs-analysis" for
<u>OUR FAMILY!</u> I don't ever recall any of those "Policy
Pushers" coming over to the house and offering to help
my grandmother "organize" the mountain of "virtually
worthless paper" that they had piled upon her and had the
audacity to call them "Life Insurance Policies!!!" Maybe
their time was "too precious" to spend a few moments
with MY FAMILY to explain what we were paying for.

That's one of the main reasons today why I want to
make sure that <u>EVERY FAMILY IN NORTH AMERICA</u> is
offered a Complimentary....No-Obligation....No Strings
Attached.... Needs Analysis......so that they can KNOW

WHERE THEY STAND. EVERY FAMILY DESERVES THAT!!

- Many years later, while I was an Agency Manager with one of the top insurance companies in America, I heard one of my agents say those same words to a client who had just called him to say that her husband had died. She stated that she wanted to delete her husband's new truck from their Auto Insurance Policy and the agent wanted to know WHY. He, too, expressed his deepest sympathy.....and repeated those same "sad and sorry" words: "If there's anything that I can do, please let me know!" I looked at him and wanted to say: "You, as their agent, should have already done what you were supposed to do in the FIRST PLACE!!!"

  I pulled the files and, to my dismay, this "multi-line agent," who called himself a PROFESSIONAL, had never offered this family the "opportunity" to secure the "financial future" of their family. This family had a history of having insurance with this "so-called" PROFESSIONAL AGENT for the last 18 years and I could not find any record, any document, any quote, or any note in those files with the word "LIFE INSURANCE" or any other document with an "L" on it. Personally, I have very little tolerance or respect for an "agent" who refuses to offer clients the "opportunity" to protect the "financial future" of their family. It doesn't matter what the client says. In my opinion, we, as PROFESSIONAL AGENTS, have a "moral obligation" to our clients to explain the risk.... And then.....to offer them an "opportunity" to transfer those risks from their family to the insurance company. Isn't that what we do? Or expected to do?

- To all of the Insurance Agents, Managers and Companies of America: "We've got lots of work to do!!!"

Travel with me, if you will, back to July, 1961. Had one of those "insurance premium collectors" thought about US and SOLD my mom a $1,000,000 Life Insurance Policy, at age 29 (for only $45 per month), do you think Life would have been a little different for her son today?

- We, as Insurance Agents, Managers and Companies of America, hold the keys to <u>"millions of tomorrows!!"</u> What we <u>DO</u>.....or <u>DON'T DO</u>.... can determine the quality of life that millions of people will experience for generations to come.

When it was all said and done, at the age of 16, I literally was forced to enter the Insurance Industry...from a different angle. In an effort to protect <u>MY</u> family....from the "insurance collectors," I was forced to learn how to read plans and policies, cash surrender value tables, etc. I called each and every one of those "insurance collectors" and had a "face to face" meeting with them to discuss my disappointment in them and what they had done to my family......and to "cash in" every policy on <u>everybody</u> but my grandmother. We used the proceeds to pay off all of my grandmother's bills and put the rest of the proceeds in a bank account for her. I also told every one of them that they were forever forbidden to come to our home again and instructed them to mail a monthly bill (which we paid with a money order) from that day forward. So we went on "direct monthly payment" immediately and never saw any one of them again.....because they knew.......that <u>WE KNEW</u>!!! Their game was over in our household.

We appreciated all the sympathy....but...being an only child...with no father in the household....we needed a <u>CHECK</u>!!

And here we are in the year 2008, and I'm still in a rage over the way that my family was "used and abused" by these "insurance premium collectors," and, to this day, I try to do everything that I can to make sure that people <u>UNDERSTAND</u> what's really going on.....what the risks are....and how to protect their family.

- As Insurance Professionals, one of the most important things that we can do is to sit down and have a "face-to face" consultation with <u>EVERY ONE OF OUR CLIENTS</u> (the people who have placed their trust in us) and do a "Free- No-Obligation Needs Analysis" for them and to offer them the "opportunity" to take action on those things that are important to them and their family. How many people in America have ever had an agent to <u>CARE ENOUGH ABOUT THEM</u> to sit down with them and show them how to put together a plan that will do the following (without expecting to make an immediate sale and a commission):

  1. Pay Off The Mortgage
  2. Send Their Kids To College

3. Pay Off All The Bills
4. Provide An On-Going Monthly Income
5. Provide Financial Expenses

- To the Insurance Agents, Managers and Companies of America, I would ask you to put a Plan Of Action In Place to offer Every Client That You Currently Have Insured And Every Prospect With Whom You Come In Contact With In The Future A "Free-No-Obligation Insurance Check-Up" just to make sure that their "financial house" is in order in the event of the premature death of the financial provider(s). For all we know, they may have been a "victim" like my family was. Remember this: We hold the keys to many futures!

Some times we do what we do.....because of what we've been through. I wanted to share the background information with you so that you could better understand some of the reasons why I'm so "passionate" about helping others avoid some of the things that my family had to go through as a result of trusting people who were more concerned about what was in it for THEM. Those unfortunate events "set the stage" for a 30 year (and counting) career, in the Insurance Industry, that has been dedicated to helping as many people as I possibly can!!!

"LIFE MADE EASY"

(Install A Life Marketing System In Your Agency)

ANY AGENT who installs a Life Marketing System and is willing to work it on a **consistent** basis will increase their life sales!!

ANY AGENT who installs a Life Marketing System and is willing to work it on a **consistent** basis will increase their life sales!!

ANY AGENT who installs a Life Marketing System and is willing to work it on a **consistent** basis will increase their life sales!!

One of the Top Life Insurance Producers gave me this advice: ***"One of the main reasons why I am one of the Top Life Insurance Producers at this company is not because of my talent or any super sales ability. It's because I have the drive...the desire... the discipline.......and a simple repeatable process that I use EVERYDAY. During the course of a week, we will encounter many clients and prospects. WATCH ME.........DUPLICATE what you see me saying and doing.....and show me two (2) Life Applications EVERY week...if you're serious!!!"*** And I'll see you at the LEADERS CONFERENCE in Bermuda!!!

Agent, W. C.
1978

I was fortunate enough to have the opportunity to work with **two** of the Top Life Insurance Producers in the company. Mr. "T" taught me how to move all of the information that I had learned in training school from my "head to my heart" and how to speak "from heart to heart" with clients and prospects. We did role plays everyday on how to **"overcome objections"** and I will share some of those with you as well. During one of the regional life contests, he sold 31 of the 32 people that he called on. He is clearly one of the best that I've ever seen!!! One of the most "touching moments" that we shared was when I asked him what to expect when we had to deliver a death claim. Both of us had tears in our eyes as he "recalled" one of those moments:

> *"I want you to imagine going over to a home and sitting down at a small kitchen table....and facing "MRS. Johnson"... who just lost her husband...... and their three little kids are sitting on the floor around you..... looking in YOUR EYES... with tears in THEIR EYES. And you remember....that you told "MR. Johnson" when you sold him the policy that...... on the day that he "stepped out"......you and your company would "step in" to help his family. AND THIS IS THAT VERY MOMENT. Everybody in the house (including YOU)....is full of tears....shaking and crying....and you ALL realize that YOU are the ONLY ONE who will be coming to the house with a CHECK to help them. And whatever YOU have for them..... is all that they'll have!! And that's why we have to continue to do WHAT WE DO...... to help as many families as we possibly can!!!"*

Agent, T. M.
1978

Agent W.C. and Agent T. M. both had their own style of delivering the message. Two very different personalities..... No.1 and 2... or No. 2 and 1 on the "Life Leader Board"....all year long.....a very close race....too close to call sometimes. Agent W.C. told me to WATCH HIM and DUPLICATE what HE was saying and doing.... And I did. Everyday.....like clock-work.....he was mailing out company-produced brochures, letters and business cards and making follow-up phone calls to set appointments and close sales..... and Agent T. M. the "master" at overcoming any and all objections..... told me to WATCH HIM and DUPLICATE what HE was saying and doing....and I did. Watching each of them interact with a client or prospect was like watching a symphony conductor and an orchestra. They both made "beautiful music!" And I was "caught" in the middle of the ACTION.....EVERYDAY. Surrounded by two of the Best Life Producers in the company....... In their finest hour!! What a way to start a career. WOW!!!!

So I "blended in" the "best" from both of them....... With what was working for me during my OWN interactions with clients and prospects and developed "LIFE MADE EASY," which helped me to join my mentors at the top of the production charts and become one of the Top Life Producers as well. I would suggest that you find the Top Producers in your District, Region, City, State or Nation and be "humble enough" to ask them to be one of your mentors. Treat them to Breakfast, Lunch or Dinner and JUST LISTEN. They'll SHARE.....if you'll LISTEN. Then TAKE ACTION!

So IF YOU'RE SERIOUS about increasing your LIFE SALES, show ME and YOUR MANAGERS...... a minimum of two life applications EVERY week. Over a

50 week period, you will generate a minimum of 100 Life Applications (<u>IF YOU'RE SERIOUS!!!</u>). And I do want to hear from YOU. My e-mail adress is located in the rear of the book.

"WHAT IS YOUR VISION OF LIFE INSURANCE?"

Life Insurance has many features and benefits and can be designed to accomplish many things...but the FIRST OBJECTIVE that I like to focus on is helping people to protect the "financial future" of their family against the loss of income due to a premature death of the "financial provider (s)" or the "CEO" of the family. As we've stated previously, if the "Chief Executive Officer" of the family is earning $100,000 per year and passes away prematurely, that family will suffer a "loss of income" of "$1,000,000 plus" in a 10 year period.........."$2,000,000 plus" in a 20 year period..... "$3,000,000 plus" in a 30 year period. How many families can afford to suffer financial losses like that? Without that income.....what happens to that family? We, as professional agents, literally, hold the "keys to their future." We know some things that they don't know......and, in my opinion, we have a moral obligation to share our knowledge with them....and to offer them an "opportunity" to protect their loved ones. It's O.K. to have more than one type of policy in the clients' portfolio to satisfy different objectives. But I like to start by helping to insure the family's income and lifestyle FIRST. So let's get started!

A Proven Life Marketing System

1. Start with a list of at least 100 clients or prospects and keep adding names to your list on a daily basis. Always keep your list at 100 plus so that you'll always have clients and prospects to interact with.
2. Prepare a Targeted Direct Mail Campaign With A

Pre-Approach Package.

- Review all of the available company-produced brochures and prospecting letters.
- Choose the brochures and prospecting letters that will deliver the message that you would like to deliver.
- Make sure that your package includes some type of "Call To Action" which will cause your prospects to return a reply card or to make contact with you to take action to protect the "financial future" of their family.

3. Start the process. In order to be successful, you must be Consistent and Persistent on a DAILY basis. Incorporate this process into your Daily Activities.

- Monday   Mail 5 Packages
- Tuesday   Mail 5 Packages
- Wednesday   Mail 5 Packages
- Thursday   Mail 5 Packages/
                            Call 5 From Monday
- Friday   Mail 5 Packages/
                            Call 5 From Tuesday
- Monday   Mail 5 Packages/
                            Call 5 From Wednesday
- Tuesday   Mail 5 Packages/
                            Call 5 From Thursday
- Wednesday   Mail 5 Packages/
                            Call 5 From Friday
- Thursday   Mail 5 Packages/
                            Call 5 From Monday
- Friday   Mail 5 Packages/

	Call 5 From Tuesday
• Monday	Mail 5 Packages/
	Call 5 From Wednesday

(How Can You Fail With All Of This Activity???)

4. Follow-up with a Phone Call. The Purpose Of The Follow-Up Phone Call Is To Set Up An Appointment To Offer and Conduct a "Free-No-Obligation Life Insurance Check Up."

<u>Suggested Word Track After The Customary Greeting:</u>

"This is _____, your _____ Insurance Agent. How are you today? I'm calling concerning the information that we sent you a few days ago. The reason that we sent the information is because we want to make sure that if something were to happen prematurely....your family would be in a position to pay off the mortgage, send your kids to college and continue to have a monthly income coming in. Is that important to you?

5. What To Expect During The Follow-Up Phone Calls: No, No, No. No, No, No, <u>Yes</u>, No, No, <u>Yes</u>, No, No, No, <u>Yes</u>, No, No, No, No. <u>Yes</u>, No, <u>Yes</u>, <u>Yes</u>, No, No, No, <u>Yes</u>, <u>Yes</u>, <u>Yes</u>, No, No, No, No, <u>Yes</u>, <u>Yes</u>, No, <u>Yes</u>

6. Complete A Free "No-Obligation" Needs Analysis for your clients and prospects so that <u>they will know</u> how much "<u>CASH MONEY</u>" their loved ones would need to do the following:

- Pay Off the Mortgage or To Buy a New Home (assuming that they are currently renting)?
- Educational Expenses for the kids?
- Income Replacement?
- To pay off all of the family bills?
- To provide an Emergency Fund?
- To provide for Final Expenses?

7. Prepare & Offer Solutions:

- Term Insurance? 10 years? 20 years? 30 years?
- Term Insurance with Return of Premium?
- Whole Life Insurance?
- Universal Life Insurance?
- A Combination of Permanent and Term Insurance?
- Offer a maximum of three (3) solutions.
- Explain the features and benefits of the each solution.....and ask the question: "Which one do <u>YOU</u> feel more comfortable with?" (as opposed to how much can you AFFORD?)

8. Overcoming Some Of The Most Common Objections:

OBJECTION NO. 1: "We Can't Afford It."

Suggested Word Track:

I know how you feel. You've got the house note, two car notes, the light bill, the phone bills, the cable bill, the food bill, the gas bill, the day care center, etc. ....and here I am...... talking about adding another bill. But there's something special about this bill. It's the only bill in your entire stack of bills that can pay off all of the other bills.....in addition to paying off the mortgage, sending your kids to college, and providing a monthly income to your family. Is that important to you?

OBJECTION NO. 2: "I Have Insurance At Work."

Suggested Work Track:

That's great! Most people do. But let me ask you a question: The insurance that you have at work......will it pay off your mortgage, send your kids to college, pay off the bills for the family, provide a monthly income for your family and pay final expenses?
(The answer will ALWAYS be NO!)

Would it be O.K. with you if we provided you with a "Free, No-Obligation Needs Analysis" so that you and your family will know how much Cash Money would be needed to protect THEIR "financial future?"

OBJECTION NO. 3: "I Need To Think About It!"

Suggested Work Track:

Great! We have a program for that. Let me show you how it works. You look good on the <u>outside</u>.....but nobody knows how you look on the **inside.**

Here's what we can do for you: We can fill out an application and send it in to our Underwriting Department to see if you can <u>qualify</u> for the policy. That process will take about 30 to 45 days. If the policy is issued, we'll get together again and deliver the policy to you for your review. You'll have another 10 days to look everything over under our "Ten Day FREE- LOOK Program." If you're not satisfied, for any reason, we'll return your deposit. So the question is: Would you rather be <u>COVERED</u> while you're thinking about it or <u>NOT COVERED</u> while you're thinking about it? Which one makes more sense to <u>YOU</u>?

OBJECTION NO. 4: "My Brother In Law Is In The Business."

Suggested Word Track:

That's great! So have you had your "Free Life Insurance Review" for the year? For example: If something were to happen to you prematurely, do you have any idea how much <u>cash</u> your family would need to (1) pay off the mortgage and keep your home in the family (2) provide the funds for your children's education (3) to pay off all the bills for the family (4) to provide an ongoing monthly income for your family and (5) to provide for final expenses? One of the services that we provide is a "Free, No-Obligation Needs Analysis and Life Insurance

Review." Would it be O.K. with you if we provided that free service for you and your family?........ because sometimes you may not want your brother-in-law to know all of your personal financial business.

9. Close The Sale

10. Obtaining Referrals:

Every human being on the planet knows at least three (3) people that you don't know. So it's important to offer <u>Exceptional Service</u> to each and every client or prospect. When you do that, they will be more willing to provide you with additional people with whom you can share your services. Your <u>Exceptional Service </u>will cause them to open up the "windows of their world" to you.....and could be a source of <u>unlimited referrals.</u>

<u>Suggested Work Track:</u>

We want to build our business with good people just like you! Our "Free, No-Obligation Needs Analysis and Life Insurance Review" is available to you....Every member of your family.....and any of your friends and associates that you recommend. Is there any body else that <u>YOU</u> care about....that you'd like me to share this "opportunity" with? You can be assured that we'll offer the same <u>Exceptional Service</u> to <u>THEM</u> that we offered to <u>YOU</u>!

11. Deliver The Policy & Set Up The Appointment For The Annual Review Next Year.

Setting the appointment a year in advance solidifies the fact that this was not just a "one-time transaction" for YOU to make a commission on THEM. It also lets them know that you intend to come back to see about them. And it won't be a surprise when you call to CONFIRM your appointment two weeks in advance of the actual date. One of the best ways to expand the relationship and to retain a client for a twenty year period....is to make sure that you continue to meet with your client each year.....for a twenty year period. If you want to have a client for LIFE, you've got to get involved in THEIR LIFE!!!

How To Generate $62,400 Per Year In Life Sales

- 25 Letters per week <u>and</u>
- 25 Follow-Up Phone Calls per week
- Should generate 5 Face To Face Appointments
- Which should generate at least 2 Sales Per Week
- If your "average annual premium" per case is <u>$600</u> ($50 per month)
- 2 sales per week @ <u>$600 Per Year</u> in Annual Premiums
- Equals $1,200 <u>Per Week</u> In Life Sales
- 52 Weeks @ 1,200 per week
- Will generate <u>$62,400</u> per year in Life Sales

How To Generate $100,000 Per Year In Life Sales

- If your "average annual premium" per case is <u>$1,000</u> ($ 84 per month)
- 2 sales per week @ <u>$1,000 Per Year</u> in Annual Premiums
- Equals $2,000 <u>Per Week</u> in Life Sales
- 52 weeks @ $2,000 per week
- Will generate $104,000 per year in Life Sales

The *"Separate Account"*

Retirement Strategy!

This Is Your Opportunity To Get Wealthy!!!

For Illustration Purposes Only

(Potential Income Will Vary Based Upon Your Actual Commission Rate)

Open A "Separate Account" To Deposit The Income From Your Life Insurance Sales

Level 1:

2 Policies Per Week @ $50 Per Month ($600 Annual Premium Per Policy) =

$1,200   Per Week In Production For 50 Weeks =
            $60,000 Per Year In Annual Premiums@ 50% =
            $30,000 Per Year In Commissions

Deposited Into A "Separate Account"
For Your Retirement

For **10** Years =

$300,000 In Extra Income.......From Your Life Sales!!

Level 2:

3 Policies Per Week @ $50 Per Month ($600 Annual Premium Per Policy) =

$1,800   Per Week In Production For 50 Weeks =
             $90,000 Per Year In Annual Premiums @ 50% =
             $45,000 Per Year In Commissions

Deposited Into A "Separate Account"
For Your Retirement

For **10** Years =

$450,000 In Extra Income........From Your Life Sales!!

Level 3:

$2,000   Per Week In Production For 50 Weeks=
             $100,000 Per Year In Annual Premiums @ 50%
             $ 50,000 Per Year In Commissions

Deposited Into A "Separate Account"
For Your Retirement

For **10** Years =

$500,000 In Extra Income…….. From Your Life Sales!!

Advice From The

$10,000,000 Per Year Producer

I want to share some very valuable information with you that I learned at my very first company-sponsored conference. At the "Presidents Conference" at The South Hampton Princess Hotel in Bermuda, I had the opportunity to meet an agent who had built an agency that was generating $10,000,000 in annual premiums. The main question that everybody wanted to ask him was "How do you build a $10,000,000 per year book of business?" And his answer was: <u>"ONE DAY AT A TIME!"</u> He built it to over $3,000,000 without the help of a CSR or any additional producers.....using paper applications and rate books.

This is what he said:

5 Key Points From
The "10,000,000" Man

- **Property & Casualty Goals**

<u>$2,000 per day</u> in <u>NEW</u> Property & Casualty Production = $10,000 per week =$520,000 per year.....at the end of three years: $1,560,000....at the end of 5 years: $2,600,000.

- **Life Insurance Goals**

$1,000 per week in Annual Life Premiums.......A minimum of $52,000 per year in Life Premiums................... each year and every year.

- Always sell <u>more than one</u> policy in <u>each</u> household .....in an effort to "solidify" the relationship with <u>each</u> client and to insulate your clients from the competition.

- Treat EACH CUSTOMER like a KING or a QUEEN.

- Expand your agency with producers who can <u>DUPLICATE</u> that pattern. Duplicate YOURSELF and SUPER-SIZE YOUR Agency!

So when I returned home, my goal was to "duplicate that pattern." I set my "Daily Production Goals" at $2,000 per day of NEW P & C premiums...$<u>10,000 per week</u> in <u>Property & Casualty Sales</u> and $<u>1,000 per week</u> in <u>Life Insurance Sales.</u> That's how the <u>2/10/1 Production Plan</u> was developed. Did I always achieve my $2,000 per day? NO!........but many times....I did. Had I not qualified to attend this conference, I NEVER WOULD HAVE RECEIVED SUCH VALUABLE INFORMATION. That's one of the main reasons why it's important for <u>YOU TO QUALIFY</u> to attend all "Leaders Conferences." At the "Leaders Conferences," you'll be surrounded by "Leaders" and the "Best In Class" and if you are willing to <u>"listen, learn and execute,"</u> that could cause tremendous growth in your agency.

That particular "Presidents Conference" took place somewhere around 1980 and I shared that same pattern, as a Territory Sales Manager, with my agents in Michigan and our team finished the year 2005 as follows:

- Auto Production   90% of Plan   #1 in East Metro Market
- Home Production 120% of Plan   #1 in East Metro Market
- Memberships   111% of Plan   #2 in East Metro Market

The actual results are included for your review...but the names of the Company, Regional Sales Director and the other Territory Sales Managers have been removed.

TSM	December YTD Auto	YTD Seasonal Target	% of Goal Achieved	December YTD Home	YTD Seasonal Target	% of Goal Achieved	December YTD Membership	YTD Seasonal Target	% of Goal Achieved
RSD	22100	26189	84%	6961	7073	98%	49298	49218	100%
TSM - A	3177	3699	86%	1063	1068	100%	6167	7252	85%
TSM - B	2621	3001	87%	846	965	88%	6312	6410	98%
TSM - C	2118	2696	79%	730	760	96%	4861	4527	107%
TSM - D	1729	2152	80%	404	353	114%	5403	6551	82%
TSM - E	3363	3885	87%	1053	1089	97%	6581	6239	105%
TSM - F	2931	3531	83%	940	969	97%	6867	6063	113%
TSM - G	2689	3380	80%	967	1073	90%	6045	5799	104%
TSM - Pierre	3472	3845	90%	958	796	120%	7062	6377	111%

So how do you build a $10,000,000 agency? <u>One Day At A Time!</u> Concentrate on all of your processes, activities, staff production requirements and expectations and set your "daily production goal" at a minimum of $2,000 per day of <u>NEW PROPERTY & CASUALTY BUSINESS</u>.....and make sure you have the processes in place to generate that $2,000 and more.... And $1,000 per week in LIFE INSURANCE SALES.

<u>LET'S TAKE A CLOSER LOOK</u>

- What Activities & Processes do you <u>currently</u> have in place to generate your Property & Casualty Sales and your Life Sales?

- How much <u>NEW</u> business are you currently producing on a daily basis? Review your Actual "Daily" Production for the next two weeks.

- What additional Activities & Processes could you add to increase your <u>Sales, Retention & Referrals</u>?

NOTES:

_____

_____

_____

_____

_____

_____

_____

_____

_____

My Action Plan

_____

_____

_____

_____

_____

_____

_____

_____

_____

_____

_____

_____

NOTES:

_____

_____

_____

_____

_____

_____

_____

_____

_____

My Action Plan

_____

_____

_____

_____

_____

_____

_____

_____

_____

_____

_____

_____

Monday

"Success On A Daily Basis"
The Multiline Advantage

Multiple Opportunities................ Multiple Income Streams

$2,000 Per Day of NEW P & C Premiums!!!

# Policies Written	Policy Type	Premium Written
_____	Auto Policies	_____
_____	Homeowners Policies	_____
_____	Fire Policies	_____
_____	Tenant Policies	_____
_____	Flood Insurance Policies	_____
_____	Commercial Auto Policies	_____
_____	Other Commercial Policies	_____
_____	Boat Insurance Policies	_____
_____	Motorcycle Policies	_____
_____	Recreational Vehicle Policies	_____
_____	Umbrella Policies	_____
_____	Scheduled Personal Property	_____
_____	Other P & C Policies	_____

Total # Policies

Total Premium Written

_____

_____

Total Produced <u>MONDAY</u>

71

NOTES:

_____
_____
_____
_____
_____
_____
_____
_____
_____

My Action Plan

_____
_____
_____
_____
_____
_____
_____
_____
_____
_____
_____

Tuesday

"Success On A Daily Basis"
The Multiline Advantage

Multiple Opportunities............... Multiple Income Streams

$2,000 Per Day of NEW P & C Premiums!!!

# Policies Written	Policy Type	Premium Written
_____	Auto Policies	_____
_____	Homeowners Policies	_____
_____	Fire Policies	_____
_____	Tenant Policies	_____
_____	Flood Insurance Policies	_____
_____	Commercial Auto Policies	_____
_____	Other Commercial Policies	_____
_____	Boat Insurance Policies	_____
_____	Motorcycle Policies	_____
_____	Recreational Vehicle Policies	_____
_____	Umbrella Policies	_____
_____	Scheduled Personal Property	_____
_____	Other P & C Policies	_____

Total # Policies   **Total Premium Written**

_____   _____

Total Produced TUESDAY

73

NOTES:

_____

_____

_____

_____

_____

_____

_____

_____

My Action Plan

_____

_____

_____

_____

_____

_____

_____

_____

_____

_____

Wednesday

"Success On A Daily Basis"
The Multiline Advantage

Multiple Opportunities................ Multiple Income Streams

$2,000 Per Day of NEW P & C Premiums!!!

# Policies Written	Policy Type	Premium Written
_____	Auto Policies	_____
_____	Homeowners Policies	_____
_____	Fire Policies	_____
_____	Tenant Policies	_____
_____	Flood Insurance Policies	_____
_____	Commercial Auto Policies	_____
_____	Other Commercial Policies	_____
_____	Boat Insurance Policies	_____
_____	Motorcycle Policies	_____
_____	Recreational Vehicle Policies	_____
_____	Umbrella Policies	_____
_____	Scheduled Personal Property	_____
_____	Other P & C Policies	_____

Total # Policies

_____

Total Premium Written

_____

Total Produced _Wednesday_

75

NOTES:

_____
_____
_____
_____
_____
_____
_____
_____
_____
_____

My Action Plan

_____
_____
_____
_____
_____
_____
_____
_____
_____
_____
_____
_____

Thursday

"Success On A Daily Basis"
The Multiline Advantage

Multiple Opportunities............... Multiple Income Streams

$2,000 Per Day of NEW P & C Premiums!!!

# Policies Written	Policy Type	Premium Written
_____	Auto Policies	_____
_____	Homeowners Policies	_____
_____	Fire Policies	_____
_____	Tenant Policies	_____
_____	Flood Insurance Policies	_____
_____	Commercial Auto Policies	_____
_____	Other Commercial Policies	_____
_____	Boat Insurance Policies	_____
_____	Motorcycle Policies	_____
_____	Recreational Vehicle Policies	_____
_____	Umbrella Policies	_____
_____	Scheduled Personal Property	_____
_____	Other P & C Policies	_____

Total # Policies

_____

Total Premium Written

_____

Total Produced Thursday

NOTES:

_____
_____
_____
_____
_____
_____
_____
_____
_____

My Action Plan

_____
_____
_____
_____
_____
_____
_____
_____
_____
_____
_____
_____

Friday

"Success On A Daily Basis"
The Multiline Advantage

Multiple Opportunities............... Multiple Income Streams

$2,000 Per Day of NEW P & C Premiums!!!

# Policies Written	Policy Type	Premium Written
_____	Auto Policies	_____
_____	Homeowners Policies	_____
_____	Fire Policies	_____
_____	Tenant Policies	_____
_____	Flood Insurance Policies	_____
_____	Commercial Auto Policies	_____
_____	Other Commercial Policies	_____
_____	Boat Insurance Policies	_____
_____	Motorcycle Policies	_____
_____	Recreational Vehicle Policies	_____
_____	Umbrella Policies	_____
_____	Scheduled Personal Property	_____
_____	Other P & C Policies	_____

Total # Policies

_____

Total Premium Written

_____

Total Produced Friday

NOTES:

_____

_____

_____

_____

_____

_____

_____

_____

_____

_____

My Action Plan

_____

_____

_____

_____

_____

_____

_____

_____

_____

_____

_____

_____

Saturday

"Success On A Daily Basis"
The Multiline Advantage

Multiple Opportunities................ Multiple Income Streams

$2,000 Per Day of NEW P & C Premiums!!!

# Policies Written	Policy Type	Premium Written
_____	Auto Policies	_____
_____	Homeowners Policies	_____
_____	Fire Policies	_____
_____	Tenant Policies	_____
_____	Flood Insurance Policies	_____
_____	Commercial Auto Policies	_____
_____	Other Commercial Policies	_____
_____	Boat Insurance Policies	_____
_____	Motorcycle Policies	_____
_____	Recreational Vehicle Policies	_____
_____	Umbrella Policies	_____
_____	Scheduled Personal Property	_____
_____	Other P & C Policies	_____

Total # Policie

_____

Total Premium Written

_____

Total Produced <u>Saturday</u>

81

NOTES:

_____
_____
_____
_____
_____
_____
_____
_____
_____
_____

My Action Plan

_____
_____
_____
_____
_____
_____
_____
_____
_____
_____
_____
_____

Today's Date

"Success On A Daily Basis"
The Multiline Advantage

Multiple Opportunities............... Multiple Income Streams

$2,000 Per Day of NEW P & C Premiums!!!

# Policies Written	Policy Type	Premium Written
_____	Auto Policies	_____
_____	Homeowners Policies	_____
_____	Fire Policies	_____
_____	Tenant Policies	_____
_____	Flood Insurance Policies	_____
_____	Commercial Auto Policies	_____
_____	Other Commercial Policies	_____
_____	Boat Insurance Policies	_____
_____	Motorcycle Policies	_____
_____	Recreational Vehicle Policies	_____
_____	Umbrella Policies	_____
_____	Scheduled Personal Property	_____
_____	Other P & C Policies	_____

Total # Policies   **Total Premium Written**

_____   _____

Total Produced TODAY

83

NOTES:

_____

_____

_____

_____

_____

_____

_____

_____

My Action Plan

_____

_____

_____

_____

_____

_____

_____

_____

_____

_____

Weekly Goal

$10,000 Per Week x 52 Weeks = $520,000!!!

Weekly Property & Casualty Premiums Produced

Total Weekly Production_____
**Divided By The No. of Days In That Week Is Your
"Daily Production Rate."**

Week # 1:   Total Production   "<u>Daily</u>" Production Rate
_____   _____

Week # 2:   Total Production   "<u>Daily</u>" Production Rate
_____   _____

Week # 3:   Total Production   "<u>Daily</u>" Production Rate
_____   _____

Week # 4:   Total Production   "<u>Daily</u>" Production Rate
_____   _____

Week # 5:   Total Production   "<u>Daily</u>" Production Rate
_____   _____

Week # 6:   Total Production   "<u>Daily</u>" Production Rate
_____   _____

Week # 7:   Total Production   "<u>Daily</u>" Production Rate
_____   _____

Week # 8:   Total Production   "<u>Daily</u>" Production Rate
_____   _____

Week # 9:   Total Production   "<u>Daily</u>" Production Rate
_____   _____

Week #10:   Total Production   "<u>Daily</u>" Production Rate
_____   _____

Week #11:   Total Production   "<u>Daily</u>" Production Rate
_____   _____

Week #12:   Total Production   "<u>Daily</u>" Production Rate
_____   _____

Total <u>P & C Premiums</u> Written This <u>Quarter</u> _____
"<u>Average</u>" Premiums Written Per Week _____(Actual)
"<u>Average</u>" <u>Per Week</u> x the next 52 Weeks _____ (Projected)

Activity......Activity......Activity

Is One Of The Most Important Keys To Success!!

Surveys Show That

10 Contacts > 3 Appointments > 1 Actual Sale

20 Contacts > 6 Appointments > 2 Actual Sales

30 Contacts > 9 Appointments > 3 Actual Sales

So how many sales per week do you want to make? What kind of ACTIVITY do you need to generate those SALES?

In Financial Services, Three (3)....$90.00 per month sales......PER WEEK (that's $1,080 per sale) will generate $3,240 per week in Life Sales and $162,000 in Annual Life Sales over a 50 Week Period.

A Fast Start

For

NEW MULTI-LINE AGENTS

Minimum Weekly Goals

50 Contacts > 15 Appointments > 5 Actual Sales

Concentrate On Auto-Home-Flood-Life

Competition for market share is fierce. Many of the major "players" in the Auto and Homeowners Insurance Market want to compare policies to see if they can save you money. In other words, they want to give you a 2nd opinion. So start offering "Complimentary-No Obligation-2nd Opinions" to all of your family, friends and associates and to all of their family, friends and associates and to all of their family, friends and associates. That would be a good starting point. And whether they buy from you or not, they know others that you need to know. So your ability to obtain REFERRALS, REFERRALS and MORE REFERRALS will be a "key component" as you move forward.

On the Auto and Home policies, most customers will want an "apples to apples" comparison quote to see if you can help them save some money. And that's understandable. So offer them a "GOOD COMPARISON

QUOTE" but also offer a "BETTER <u>VALUE</u> QUOTE" with the focus on <u>VALUE</u>....so that they can also compare the "COMPARISON QUOTE" to the "BETTER VALUE QUOTE." After explaining the features and benefits of both of the policies, and what would happen in the event of a claim, ask this question:

<u>"WHICH POLICY WOULD YOU RATHER HAVE IN FORCE ON THE DAY THAT YOU HAVE TO FILE A CLAIM?"</u>
Most folks want to save money at the point of sale.....but when they have to file a claim, they want the broadest coverage possible. In many cases, the "cheapest" <u>PRICE</u> on the "front end" can lead to a disaster on the "back-end." If that client is in an At-Fault Accident and is faced with a $95,000 Judgment, that 25/50/25 policy with the "cheap price" was not the one to buy. They will begin to understand why you offered them the 100/300/100 policy as the "BETTER VALUE POLICY." At that point, they will understand the real difference between the "quote-happy agent or CSR" and a "Professional Insurance Consultant!!

<u>Flood Policies</u>:

On the Flood Policies, the question is: "Do they have the right Coverage and the right deductibles on the Dwelling and the Contents?" If they had eight feet of water in their home, would those coverages be sufficient at THAT TIME?

Life Policies:

Offer a "Complimentary-No-Obligation Needs Analysis" and an "opportunity" to protect the financial future of their family.

Retention:

If you want to keep your <u>Homeowners & Flood Insurance Policies</u> in force for the entire 20 to 30 years that the mortgage is running, be prepared to do Annual Reviews and nurture the relationships for 20 to 30 years. Each one of those accounts may have a $60,000+ value to your agency over a 20 to 30 year period.

Let's take a look at the "compounding effect" of Auto Insurance......and the value to your agency:

January	Renews in July
February	Renews in August
March	Renews in September
April	Renews in October
May	Renews in November
June	Renews in December

• •

New Business

Jan.	5 Auto Sales Per Week @ $650 For Six Months = 20 Sales
Feb.	5 Auto Sales Per Week @ $650 For Six Months = 20 Sales
Mar.	5 Auto Sales Per Week @ $650 For Six Months = 20 Sales
April	5 Auto Sales Per Week @ $650 For Six Months = 20 Sales
May	5 Auto Sales Per Week @ $650 For Six Months = 20 Sales
June	5 Auto Sales Per Week @ $650 For Six Months = 20 Sales

• •

New Business + Renewals

July	5 New Auto Sales Per Week =20 Per Month + 20 Renewals
Aug.	5 New Auto Sales Per Week =20 Per Month + 20 Renewals
Sept.	5 New Auto Sales Per Week =20 Per Month + 20 Renewals
Oct.	5 New Auto Sales Per Week =20 Per Month + 20 Renewals
Nov.	5 New Auto Sales Per Week =20 Per Month + 20 Renewals
Dec.	5 New Auto Sales Per Week =20 Per Month + 20 Renewals

• •

The above example is for illustration purposes only.....
and assumes a 100% Retention Rate. Apply your Actual
Retention Rate to the illustration.

July	40 Policies per month @ $650 = $26,000 Per Month-Auto Sales
Aug.	40 Policies per month @ $650 = $26,000 Per Month-Auto Sales
Sept.	40 Policies per month @ $650 = $26,000 Per Month-Auto Sales
Oct.	40 Policies per month @ $650 = $26,000 Per Month-Auto Sales
Nov.	40 Policies per month @ $650 = $26,000 Per Month-Auto Sales
Dec.	40 Policies per month @ $650 = $26,000 Per Month-Auto Sales

12 Months Later

New Business (NB) + Renewals (RB)

Jan   20 New Sales Per Month @ $650 = $13,000 (NB) + $26,000 (RB)=

$39,000 Per Month

Feb.   20 New Sales Per Month @ $650 = $13,000 (NB) + $26,000 (RB)=

$39,000 Per Month

Mar   20 New Sales Per Month @ $650 = $13,000 (NB) + $26,000 (RB)=

$39,000 Per Month

Apr.   20 New Sales Per Month @ $650 = $13,000 (NB) + $26,000 (RB)=

$39,000 Per Month

May   20 New Sales Per Month @ $650 = $13,000 (NB) + $26,000 (RB)=

$39,000 Per Month

June 20 New Sales Per Month @ $650 = $13,000 (NB) + $26,000 (RB)=

$39,000 Per Month

A Fresh Start For Experienced MULTI-LINE AGENTS

What additional Activities & Processes can you add to increase your Sales, Retention & Referrals?

- **Tap Into The FORTUNE IN YOUR BOOK OF BUSINESS!**

  1. There's a Fortune at your Fingertips. Review EVERY HOUSEHOLD in your book of business and "round out" the account. Make every effort to insure that <u>YOU</u> have the Auto-Home-Life and Flood Accounts in <u>YOUR</u> agency. It makes no "economic" sense to have <u>YOUR CLIENTS</u> buying products that YOU OFFER from other agents. Three and Four Agents in one household creates a "ball of confusion" for all parties involved. Somebody has to step up to the plate and eliminate the need for the other agents in that household. That's one of the reasons why it's so important to build a "relationship of trust" with each client.

  2. Run a list of Auto Clients without Home or Life.... and a list of Homeowner Clients without Auto or Flood.....and a list of Auto and Homeowner Clients without LIFE and start a targeted Direct Mail program with Follow-Up Phone Calls to increase your Daily Activities. Change the "culture" in the agency from Defense To Offense!

- **Duplicate The Postal Service and the Restaurant Industry's "Cross-Selling Philosophy" In Your Agency**

1. At the end of <u>EVERY</u> transaction at the Post Office, the question is "Do you need some STAMPS today?" Every customer hears the same question EVERY TIME. Some say YES....and some say NO. By asking <u>EVERY CUSTOMER.... EVERY TIME,</u> Stamp Sales INCREASE.

2. When you go to a "Fast Food" Restaurant and order a hamburger, the "cross-sell" questions are as follows:

    Would you like some fries with that?

    Would you like to super size your order?

    Would you like a hot apple pie?

    Would you like the combo?

    By asking <u>EVERY CUSTOMER... EVERY TIME</u>, Combo Sales, Fries, Pies, Super Size Sales will all show an INCREASE.

3. When you go to a "regular restaurant," the "cross-sell" questions are as follows:

    Can we start you off with an "appetizer?"

    What can we get you to drink?

Our "specials for the day" are X.....Y....and Z.

Did you save some room for dessert?

Would you like some coffee?

By asking EVERY CUSTOMER.... EVERY TIME, Appetizer Sales, Drink Sales, Dessert Sales, Coffee Sales, the "Specials for the Day" Sales and the regular entrée sales will all show an INCREASE.

- ## So what's on YOUR MENU OF PRODUCTS & SERVICES?

1. Auto Policies
2. Homeowners Policies
3. Life & Financial Services
4. Fire Policies
5. Tenant Policies
6. Flood Insurance Policies
7. Commercial Auto Policies
8. Other Commercial Policies
9. Boat Insurance Policies
10. Motorcycle Policies
11. Recreational Vehicle Policies
12. Umbrella Policies
13. Scheduled Personal Property
14. P & C Policies
15. Complimentary Needs-Analysis
16. Complimentary Policy Reviews

Does everybody on your staff understand the importance of Cross-Selling? Have you created a "Cross-Selling" culture in your agency? What question is being asked of EVERY ONE OF YOUR CLIENTS.......EVERY TIME?

• <u>Create An Agency-Level Newsletter</u>

Introduce your team (with photos and contact information) to your clients. Who is the Auto Insurance Specialist in the agency? Who is the Homeowners Insurance Specialist in the agency? Who is the Customer Service Representative? Who handles Claims? Who is the Flood Insurance Specialist? Publish your "Menu" of Products & Services so that clients will know what <u>YOUR</u> agency has to offer. Include a "Complimentary Needs-Analysis Form" in every edition in an effort to "increase awareness" of the need to insure the Family's INCOME. Offer "Complimentary Reviews" of all of their other policies as well......because every time that I look at another policy, I can find ways to "improve" it and, perhaps, offer a better VALUE.

Partner with several restaurants in your market whereby you will allow them to advertise in your newsletter if they are willing to offer YOUR clients a "Buy One.... Get One Free....Breakfast- Lunch or Dinner." Share photos of Community Events that you and your team participated in. Show your team in "Action" in the community. Use your newsletter to "educate" your clients on different policies. For example, what is a Personal Umbrella Policy? What are the features and benefits of a Personal Umbrella Policy? What are the features and benefits of an Auto Policy? A Homeowners Policy? A Flood Insurance Policy? Etc. Is the CHEAPEST PRICE ALWAYS the BEST PRICE? Talk about your great Claims

Service. Give examples of what can happen when the proper coverages are not in place. Don't get involved in POLITICS in your newsletter. Gather e-mail addresses for your client database. Start a Referral Network within your Newsletter. For every person that they refer to your agency, you can enter their name into a drawing. Once a month, you will name a winner......and have a variety of prizes.....like a $50 Gift Card...a $25 Gift Card...... Dinner for Two at a nice restaurant, a ticket to an NFL game, a "free oil change" coupon, etc. You also want to create an online version. Send your newsletter out to all of your clients on a Quarterly basis......Winter...Spring.... Summer and Fall Editions. In addition to Restaurants, partner with Auto Service Companies and other Service Contractors and have them advertise in your newsletter with coupons for Oil Changes, A/C Check Ups, Meals, etc. Make it an exciting "interactive" newsletter. Talk about the importance of Annual Reviews. Stay "connected" to your clients and, by all means, make sure that your clients AND PROSPECTS stay "connected" to you and your agency.

• Water <u>YOUR</u> Garden. "A Bird In The Hand Is Worth Two In The Bush!"

Some agents spend more money and other resources chasing "new prospects" as opposed to "watering the garden" that they already have. My focus was always on the ones that I already had "in the house." My grandmother used to always say that "A Bird in the Hand Is Worth Two in the Bush!" Cultivate the relationships with the ones that you already have. They ALL need AUTO-HOME-LIFE and FLOOD with <u>YOUR AGENCY!</u> And, in many cases, you may only have the Auto Policy while the Home,

Life and Flood Policies may be with three other agents. "Sweep" the other agents out of YOUR HOUSEHOLDS and "purify" the house. Too many agents.....too many opinions....too much confusion. If you currently have 2,000 Households....... Each with one (1) Policy in Force, what would happen.....if you could "bring over" one (1) additional policy in each of those 2,000 households. That would double your Policies in Force to 4,000. And since you already have the "foundation" for the relationship, why not expand that relationship? That's what I mean when I say "Water YOUR Garden."

Offer "Complimentary 2nd Opinions" On All Lines Because Almost Every time That You Review A Policy With A Client or Prospect, You Will Find A GAP In The Coverages. And The Question Is:

"Which Policy Would You Rather Have In Force On The Day That You Have To File A Claim?"

• Commercial Auto

During a Commercial Auto training class, one of the speakers was the top Commercial Auto Producer in the region. When asked about the "keys" to his success, he stated the following:

1. Open your "eyes" and become "aware" of your surroundings and all of the Commercial Vehicles that pass you on a "daily" basis or while you are sitting in traffic......or while they are sitting in traffic.
2. Keep a voice-activated recorder at your fingertips or have an ink pen and a yellow pad on the

passenger seat of your car for the times when you are "stuck" in traffic. That's a great time to PROSPECT.

3. Most of the Commercial Vehicles will have the name of the business and the phone number of the business right there on the vehicle. Capture that information for your files.

5. <u>Inspect the vehicle</u> and the driving habits of the driver during the initial observation. The company may have one (1) vehicle for the business or 101 vehicles. That one vehicle may be a part of a very "clean" fleet of commercial vehicles.

6. When you return to your office, review your underwriting guidelines to determine if that type of vehicle is a desirable risk for your company.

7. If so.....make contact with the company and offer them a <u>COMPLIMENTARY 2nd opinion</u> on their Commercial Insurance needs. If you have a Company-Produced Commercial Auto Brochure, I suggest sending that FIRST along with your business card. A few days later, make contact.

That's the process that he used to become one of the Top Commercial Auto Producers in the region and in the company!

- ## **Private Passenger Auto**

How Can I Increase My Auto Insurance Sales?

INTERACT WITH AS MANY PEOPLE AS POSSIBLE!!

When I first started in the business, I was with a company whose message was:

Let's Compare Policies

Perhaps xxxxxx Can Save You Some Money!

The goal was to <u>interact</u> with as many people as possible and to offer them a "Complimentary-No-Obligation Review" of the policies. We wanted to offer them a 2<u>nd</u> <u>Opinion</u>. And EVERYTIME we reviewed a policy, we would seek ways to offer them a better VALUE. Almost EVERY POLICY presented an OPPORTUNITY to do that. Not only would I COMPARE the "apples to the apples quote" as they had requested, I would also offer them an "apples to a grapefruit" quote with some additional protection, features and benefits. Instead of the 25/50/10 policy....let's consider 100/300/100. After that comparison, here's the closing statement:

"Which one of those policies would you prefer to have in place <u>ON THE DAY YOU HAVE TO FILE A CLAIM?</u>"

• **Start A Cross Tell-Cross Sell Campaign**

1. I would suggest the Cross-TELL /Cross-SELL Process. Send a Company-Produced Auto Insurance Brochure (because it's Compliance-Approved)...with your business card....and then make CONTACT with your client. TELL THEM FIRST.......then CROSS SELL. That's the process that I used to let clients know, IN ADVANCE, what I wanted to talk to them about. If you LISTEN CAREFULLY during the follow-up phone call, you will be able to determine their "level of interest" by the "tones, rhythms and responses" in the clients' voice. Even if they don't buy at that particular time, you have made them "aware" of your services and have "planted a seed" for a future harvest.

2. Send Direct Mail to your TARGET MARKET with a CALL TO ACTION that will "encourage" clients and prospects to CONTACT YOU for a "Complimentary 2nd Opinion" on their Auto Insurance needs.

3. Make follow-up phone calls to those who are NOT on the Do Not Call List to offer them a "2nd Opinion" on their Auto Insurance.

4. Cross Tell and then Cross-Sell your current Homeowner Clients.

5. Cross Tell and then Cross-Sell your current Tenant Policy Holders.

6. Cross Tell and then Cross-Sell your current Boat Owner Clients.

7. <u>Cross Tell and then Cross-Sell</u> your current Motorcycle Owner Clients.

8. <u>Cross Tell and then Cross-Sell</u> your current Life Insurance Clients.

9. <u>Cross Tell and then Cross-Sell</u> EVERY CLIENT in your current book of business because they're buying it from <u>SOMEBODY</u>......so why not buy it from <u>YOU</u>?

When given the opportunity, HELP your client or prospect to determine their needs......... by <u>EXPLAINING THE COVERAGES AND OPTIONS</u> in "Plain, Easy to Understand Language." A QUOTE is just a QUOTE! But what is 50/100/50? What is 100/300/100? How does it work when there's an accident? What does it mean and what will it do for the client or prospect? What is Uninsured Motorist Coverage? What does it mean? What will it do? What's the benefit to the client or prospect? What is Collision Insurance? What is Comprehensive Insurance? What is Towing & Labor? What will it do for the client or prospect? What is Rental Reimbursement? What will it do for the client or prospect? What's in it for THEM? That's what THEY want to know! Use The Inform-Advise-Quote-Close System.

Many of your current Homeowner-Tenant-Boat Owner-Motorcycle Owner and Life clients may not even be aware of the fact that you offer <u>Auto Insurance</u> because during their "initial transaction," the main focus was on the policy that they originally purchased from your agency. A client recently told me that they had not seen or talked to their agent in the last six (6) years!!! What kind of

RELATIONSHIP does THAT AGENT have with THAT CLIENT? I would say NONE!

Build an Auto Insurance Referral Network

1. Have you introduced yourself, your agency and the features and benefits of your company's Auto Insurance Policy to the <u>SALES MANAGERS</u> at the Auto Dealerships in your market? My network consisted of 9 Auto Dealerships and 22 Auto Sales Agents who had my telephone number on SPEED DIAL!

2. Send a Company-Produced Auto Insurance Brochure....with your business card....to every Auto Dealership in your market. Then make CONTACT with the <u>SALES MANAGERS</u> (New Car Sales & Used Car Sales).

3. Include a note that states: "If we can be of service to you and your clients, please give us a call. Thanks, in advance, for giving us an opportunity to serve YOU!"

Can you think of three (3) processes that you are not currently using that you can add to your daily activities to increase your Auto Sales?

1.
2.
3.

• __Homeowners Insurance__

__How Can I Increase My Homeowner__
__Insurance Sales?__

1. Again, I would suggest the <u>Cross-TELL/ Cross-SELL Process.</u> Send a Company-Produced Homeowners Insurance Brochure....with your business card....and then make CONTACT with your client. If an interview is granted, half the sale is already done!

2. Send Direct Mail to your TARGET MARKET with a CALL TO ACTION that will "encourage" clients and prospects to CONTACT YOU for a "Complimentary 2nd Opinion" on their Homeowners Insurance needs.

3. Make follow-up phone calls to those who are NOT on the Do Not Call List to offer them a 2nd Opinion on their Homeowners Insurance.

4. <u>Cross Tell and then Cross-Sell</u> your current Auto Clients.

5. <u>Cross Tell and then Cross-Sell</u> your current Boat Owner Clients.

6. <u>Cross Tell and then Cross-Sell</u> your current Motorcycle Owner Clients.

7. <u>Cross Tell and then Cross-Sell</u> your current Life Insurance Clients.

8. Cross Tell and then Cross-Sell EVERY CLIENT in your current book of business....because they're buying it from SOMEBODY......so why not buy it from YOU?

When the opportunity presents itself, HELP the client or prospect to determine what their needs are by EXPLAINING THE COVERAGES and THE OPTIONS in "Plain Easy to Understand Language." What is Loss of Use? What's the difference between the Dwelling and the Other Structures? Most clients and prospects have never had a course in Basic Insurance....so what is Personal Liability? Replacement Cost Protection? What does all of that REALLY MEAN and what will it do for the client or prospect? Use the Inform-Advise-Quote-Close System

Many of your current Auto-Boat Owner-Motorcycle Owner and Life clients may not even be aware of the fact that you offer Homeowners Insurance because during their "initial transaction," the main focus was on the policy that they originally purchased from your agency.

Build A Homeowners Insurance Referral Network

1. Have you introduced yourself, your agency and the features and benefits of your company's Homeowners Insurance Policy to the Real Estate Agents, Mortgage Brokers, Mortgage Bankers and Closing Agents in your market? My Homeowners Referral Network consisted of 7 of the Top Real Estate Agents in the city. And for each client that they referred to me, in most cases, I sold, at least,

three policies at the initial point of sale: (a) The Homeowners Policy (b) a Flood Insurance Policy and (3) the Mortgage Cancellation Policies to protect the financial interest of our clients.

2. Send a Company-Produced Homeowners Insurance Brochure....with your business card....to the Real Estate Agents, Mortgage Brokers, Mortgage Bankers and Closing Agents in your market with a note that says: "If we can be of service to you and your clients, please give us a call. Thanks, in advance, for giving us an opportunity to serve YOU!"

3. Set up a monthly series of Home Buyers Seminars where you and your agency will be featured as the "experts" on Homeowners and Flood Insurance....... and your partners will be the"experts" on the Loan Process, the Closing Process, How to Set Up A Family Budget, the steps to take to get Pre-Approved for conventional loans and how to avoid sub-prime mortgage companies, interest only loans, balloon notes, other mortgage scams, other frauds, etc.

Can you think of three (3) processes that you are not currently using that you can add to your daily activities to increase your Homeowners Insurance Sales?

1.
2.
3.

• **Boat Owners Insurance**

One of my "20 year clients" got started at a Boat Dealership. One of the Sales Managers called and told me that he had a customer who needed a quote on some Boat Insurance. That one Boat Policy....started a "relationship" that produced the following policies in one household:

1. One Homeowners Policy
2. One Boat Policy
3. A Three (3) Car Auto Insurance Policy
4. Six (6) Landlord Policies For His Rental Properties
5. Seven (7) Flood Insurance Policies
6. Two $500,000 Life Insurance Policies
7. A 20+ Year Relationship!!!

Build A Boat Insurance Referral Network

1. Have you introduced yourself, your agency and the features and benefits of your company's Boat Insurance Policy to the Sales Managers at EVERY Boat Dealership in your city? Who else is doing that?

2. Send a Company-Produced Boat Owners Insurance Brochure....with your business card....to every Boat Dealership in your market. Then make CONTACT with the Sales Manager.

3. Include a note that states: "If we can be of service to you and your clients, please give us a call. Thanks, in advance, for giving us an opportunity to serve YOU!"

4. When you get that opportunity: <u>EXPLAIN THE COVERAGE OPTIONS in "Plain, Easy To Understand Language"- Use The Inform-Advise-Quote-Close System</u>

5. Are you advertising your services in the Specialty Magazines that target this market?

6. If you see a boat parked in the driveway of a home on a <u>consistent</u> basis, you may want to obtain the address of that property and then send a brochure to that home.....to advertise your services.

7. How many of your current clients own a Boat that may be insured with another carrier.....and another agent.....because they had no idea that you could offer them insurance for their boat? What happens to the business that YOU have in the household if the "other" agent "wakes up" and start cross selling YOUR CLIENT? But then again....who is the REAL AGENT anyway?...........
    ....<u>YOU </u>(with your one policy in the household) or the <u>OTHER AGENT</u> (with the one policy in the household)?

Can you think of three (3) processes that you are not currently using that you can add to your daily activities to increase your Boat Owners Sales?

1.
2.
3.

• **Motorcycle Insurance**

Clients and prospects who own Motorcycles also own or rent Homes or Apartments that need to be insured and have Jewelry, Watches and Furs that need to be insured........ and "people" who live in their households who are need of Life & Financial Services.

Build A Motorcycle Insurance Referral Network

1. Have you introduced yourself, your agency and the features and benefits of your company's Motorcycle Insurance Policy to the Sales Managers at EVERY Motorcycle Dealership in your city? Who else takes the time to do that? So where is the competition?

2. Send a Company-Produced Motorcycle Insurance Owners Brochure....with your business card.... to every Motorcycle Dealership in your market. Then make CONTACT with the Sales Manager.

3. Include a note that states: "If we can be of service to you and your clients, please give us a call. Thanks, in advance, for giving us an opportunity to serve YOU!"

4. When you get that opportunity: EXPLAIN THE COVERAGE OPTIONS in "Plain, Easy To Understand Language"- Use The Inform-Advise-Quote-Close System

5. Are you advertising your services in the Specialty Magazines that target this market?

6. If you see a motorcycle parked in the driveway of a home on a <u>consistent</u> basis, you may want to obtain the address of that property and then send a brochure to that home. That's a good way to say "Hello....I'm Ready...Willing...and Able to serve you." And it's a good way to "start" the relationship.

7. How many of your <u>current</u> clients own a Motorcycle that may be insured with another carrier because they are not aware of the fact that you can offer them Motorcycle Insurance as well?

Can you think of three (3) processes that you are not currently using that you can add to your daily activities to increase your Motorcycle Owners Insurance Sales?

1.
2.
3.

• __Tenants Insurance__

Clients and prospects who rent Apartments TODAY may be Homeowners TOMORROW! And most of them have Autos, Motorcycles, Boats, Jewelry, Watches, and Furs that may need to be insured NOW!........ and "people" who live in their households who probably need LIFE INSURANCE RIGHT AWAY!

__Build A Tenants Insurance Referral Network__

1. Have you introduced yourself, your agency and the features and benefits of your company's Tenants Insurance Policy to the Managers of the "Most Attractive & Desirable" Apartment Communities in your city?

2. Send a Company-Produced Tenants Insurance Brochure with your business card....to all of the "Major and Desirable" Apartment Communities in your city. Then make CONTACT with the Apartment Managers in an effort to "start" a strong working relationship.

3. Include a note in your package that states: "If we can be of service to you and your clients, please give us a call. Thanks, in advance, for giving us an opportunity to serve YOU!"

4. When you get that opportunity: EXPLAIN THE COVERAGE OPTIONS in "Plain, Easy To Understand Language"- Use The Inform-Advise-Quote-Close System

5. Are you advertising your services in the Monthly Newsletters that are being delivered directly to each tenant's door?

6. Send a Company-Produced Tenants Insurance Brochure, along with your business card and a "sample" $25,000- $35,000 or $40,000 quote to EVERY TENANT in the community.

7. How many of your current AUTO clients, who are TENANTS, have received a cross-sell letter, a brochure, a quote or direct mail from your agency informing them that (a) you offer Tenants Insurance and (b) that by adding another policy to the household, they may qualify for a multi-policy discount?

8. How many of your CURRENT clients have their Tenants Insurance Policy with another carrier because you did not give them an opportunity to buy it from YOU? Who is the REAL AGENT in that household?

9. Partner with the Apartment Managers, Police & Fire Departments and set up a series of Quarterly Crime Watch/Crime & Fire Prevention Seminars where the other "experts" will discuss ways to reduce crime and fires and other solutions to protect THEMSELVES while YOU will position yourself as the "expert" on how to protect their ASSETS. Start with one or two of the best Apartment Communities in your city and continue to expand your network until you have a network of 10 to 20 Communities. Tenants Insurance is

required in many communities today and they have to buy it from SOMEBODY......so why not buy it from <u>YOU</u>?

Can you think of three (3) processes that you are not currently using that you can add to your daily activities to increase your Tenant Insurance Sales?

1.
2.
3.

• **Umbrella Policies**

Most of your clients will have a <u>NEED</u> for a <u>PERSONAL UMBRELLA POLICY</u> but may not know <u>how to ask</u> for an Umbrella Policy or what to even ask for since this is not a product that is heavily advertised. Let's not <u>ASSUME</u> that <u>EVERY CLIENT OR PROSPECT</u> knows what a <u>"PUP"</u> is (as "insiders" like to call it). The ones "on the OUTSIDE" (our clients and prospects) may not have a CLUE what a "PUP" is…..and, unfortunately, may not find out what it is….until AFTER A LOSS that could have been covered under that policy. When I first started in the business, I had to ask somebody what a "PUP Policy" was and find out what the requirements were to put one in place. At any rate, once I found out what it was and how it works, I was in a position to explain it….. and once the client/prospect understands the nature and the need for the product, they will be more inclined to buy that <u>EXTRA LAYER OF LIABILITY</u> <u>PROTECTION.</u> You may want to include a Company-Produced Brochure that details the features and benefits of having a <u>PERSONAL UMBRELLA POLICY</u> in your monthly Direct Mail Program…..and then make a follow-up phone call to discuss with your client. It's another reason to MAKE CONTACT and to make a "good impression" while offering some very valuable information. They may not buy it during the initial call….but you will have "planted the seed" for a future harvest!

When you get an opportunity to have a "consultation" with them: <u>EXPLAIN THE COVERAGE OPTIONS in "Plain, Easy to Understand Language"- Use the Inform-Advise-Quote-Close System</u>

<u>Do you currently have a PROCESS in place to consistently promote UMBRELLA POLICIES?</u>

• Flood Insurance:

1. Inform
    Send A Flood Insurance Brochure Explaining The Risk.

2. Advise

3. Offer
    Send An Actual Quote With Your Business Card

4. Document Your Files.

• Do you offer Flood Insurance to ALL of your clients? If not, you SHOULD.....because EVERYONE LIVES IN A FLOOD ZONE!! And Homeowners Policies exclude Flooding. Our job, as agents, is to INFORM, ADVISE and OFFER our clients the opportunity to transfer risks from their family to the insurance company. Even if a flood policy is not one of the requirements for a mortgage loan, "inform.....advise.....and offer" your clients the opportunity to protect their financial interests against FLOOD LOSSES! Where are the mortgage companies and lenders who may have "read" a flood map and ADVISED homebuyers in New Orleans that they did not live in a flood zone and did not need flood insurance? Where were they, on August, 29, 2005, when Hurricane Katrina came to town? Where are they NOW? When it comes to insurance, that's our job and our profession!! Don't let the mortgage companies and lenders control whether or not you offer flood insurance to your clients. Just so you know..............

What is Flood?

Flood insurance covers direct physical loss caused by "flood." In simple terms, a flood is an excess of water on land that is normally dry. Here's the "official" definition used by the NATIONAL FLOOD INSURANCE PROGRAM.

A flood is "a general and temporary condition of partial or complete Inundation of two or more acres of normally dry land area or of two or more properties (at least one of which is your property) from:

- Overflow of inland or tidal waters;
- Unusual and rapid accumulation or runoff of surface waters from any source;
- Mudflow (which is defined as " a river of liquid and flowing mud on the surfaces of normally dry land areas, as when earth is carried by a current of water...."
- Collapse or subsidence of land along the shore of a lake or similar body of water as a result of erosion or undermining caused by waves or currents of water exceeding anticipated cyclical levels that result in a flood as defined above."

ALL OF YOUR CLIENTS need FLOOD INSURANCE. In addition to being a very valuable service to offer to your clients, you can also reduce your E & O Exposure by Offering and Selling Flood Insurance to your clients. Include a Flood Insurance Brochure in your monthly Direct Mail package and then make a follow-up phone to discuss. There's a BIG difference between an "order-

taking agent" and a "Professional Insurance Consultant."
Which one are you? Which one do you want to be?

Do you currently have a PROCESS in place to consistently promote FLOOD INSURANCE?

- **Do you currently have a PROCESS in place to consistently promote LIFE POLICIES? If not, "Activate" The Life Insurance Department In Your Agency and your Life Sales will increase!**

So Where Are You NOW... With Your Life Insurance Sales?

And Where Do You WANT TO BE?

The Power Of One

ONE (1) Life Sale Per Week x 52 Weeks = 52 Life Sales For The Year!!

Upon completion of an Auto Insurance sale, Homeowners Insurance sale, Tenants Insurance sale, Commercial Insurance sale, a Service request, or any other service, make a "smooth transition" to the Life conversation as follows:

Suggested Word Track To Cross Sell:

"I'd also like to share some information with you on one of the **MOST IMPORTANT POLICIES** that *"OUR COMPANY"* has to offer. It's the policy that can insure the family's income. Is that important to you?

At that point, you should be able to determine THEIR LEVEL OF INTEREST in protecting the "financial future" of THEIR FAMILY.

Where There's **Life**.......*There's* **Hope***!!!!*

LIFE SALES

Life Sales	#Policies Sold	#Annual Premiums
Week No. 1 Life Sales	_____	_____
Week No. 2 Life Sales	_____	_____
Week No. 3 Life Sales	_____	_____
Week No. 4 Life Sales	_____	_____
Week No. 5 Life Sales	_____	_____
Week No. 6 Life Sales	_____	_____
Week No. 7 Life Sales	_____	_____
Week No. 8 Life Sales	_____	_____
Week No. 9 Life Sales	_____	_____
Week No.10 Life Sales	_____	_____
Week No.11 Life Sales	_____	_____
Week No.12 Life Sales	_____	_____

Total Life Premiums Written This Quarter _____

"Average" Life Premiums Written Per Week _____
(Actual Production)

"Average" Per Week x the next 52 Weeks _____
(Projected Production)

NOTES:

_____
_____
_____
_____
_____
_____
_____
_____
_____

My Action Plan

_____
_____
_____
_____
_____
_____
_____
_____
_____
_____
_____
_____

Insulate Your Clients From The Competition

If YOU had a choice, would you prefer to deal with one PROFESSIONAL INSURANCE CONSULTANT and one (1) insurance company for all of your insurance needs or three (3) or more "order-taking agents" and three (3) or more insurance companies? I can tell you, from experience, that most clients would prefer to have their Auto, Home & Life with one (1) Professional Insurance Consultant (that they can depend on for sound advice and guidance)........ and one (1) insurance company. In many households, the Auto Insurance is with one agent/carrier......while the Homeowners Insurance may be with another agent/carrier and who knows where the Life Insurance is (because many "agents" are afraid to talk to their clients about insuring the "family's income" and protecting the "financial future" of their loved ones). In a case where the Auto, Home and Life Policies are all in different places, there's no "unity" in the household. So, who is the "real agent" in that household? Clients will find themselves in a position where they'll be receiving advice from one agent..... that is contrary to the advice that's being received from the other agent....... That's totally contradictory to the advice that they may be receiving from all of the other agents in the household. It's a "Ball of Confusion!"

Too Many Chefs In The Kitchen

When you have a situation like that, there are too many "Chefs" in the kitchen............... with too many different policies and policy jackets, choices, payment plans, opinions, claims numbers to remember and so many different corporate philosophies, logos and colors that it's virtually impossible for a client to develop a solid relationship or any loyalty to any of the agents or carriers involved.

Not too long ago, if you wanted (1) local and long distance phone service (2) cable service and (3) internet service, you had to order those services from three or four different providers. Nowadays, you can order ALL of those services from ONE (1) provider at a "special discounted rate" of $99 per month!

If you are a multi-line "professional"....and would like to INCREASE (1) Retention (2) Market Share and (3) Profitability..... why not use the same philosophy? Sell more than one policy in EACH of your households. As a matter of fact, if it is your goal to be the Exclusive Provider of insurance in that household, go for the "Basic Three" ...AUTO-HOME-LIFE and complete what we call the "Basic Circle of Protection," because most households have an Auto, a Home, Apartment or a Condo......and, if they are still living and breathing, will need Life Insurance?

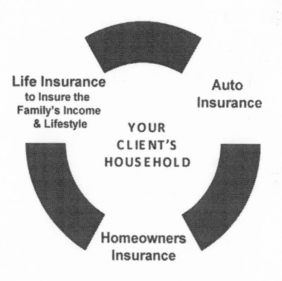

Life Insurance
to Insure the
Family's Income
& Lifestyle

Auto
Insurance

YOUR
CLIENT'S
HOUSEHOLD

Homeowners
Insurance

Failure to complete the "Basic Circle of Protection" in EACH household......is like running your computer "without security" software to protect against viruses, worms, Trojans, etc. Competitors are "FISHING" 24/7 for new customers to increase their market share.... by using cutting-edge multi-media technology and marketing techniques. So you MUST build SOLID RELATIONSHIPS with your clients and create a "FIREWALL OF PROTECTION" around your current and future households to "INSULATE" your clients from the competition!!!

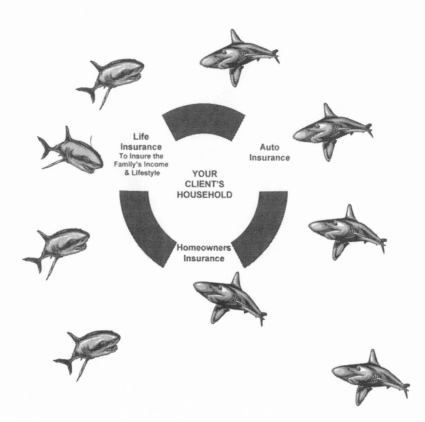

Consider the "Economic Impact" of Selling The "Basic Three" in EACH household:

Agent 1 (The "Mono-Line" Specialist)

2,000 <u>"Auto-Only"</u> Clients.....each paying $800 every six months ($1,600 per year) will generate <u>$3,200,000</u> in Annual Premiums.....
with NO LOYALITY in ANY of those households

Agent 2: (The "Multi-Line" Specialist)

2,000 Auto Clients......each paying $800 every six months ($1,600 per year) will generate <u>$3,200,000</u> in Annual Premiums from the Auto Insurance Sales.

PLUS

1000 Homeowner Clients (as a result of the cross-selling processes).. each paying $1,000 per year will generate an additional <u>$1,000,000</u> from the Homeowners Insurance Sales.

PLUS

500 Life Insurance Clients......each paying $80 per month ($960 per year) will generate <u>$480,000</u> in Life Insurance Premiums. Once you ADD LIFE into a household, that's like "locking the door" and "throwing away the key!"

In most cases, there will be three "basic windows" available for you to enter the household. If you enter through the "HOMEOWNERS" window, you may want to design a LIFE POLICY to insure the "family's income" and also offer them a "2nd Opinion" on the "AUTO" insurance as well. If you enter through the "AUTO" window, you may want to design a LIFE POLICY to insure the "family's income" and also offer them a "2nd Opinion" on the "HOMEOWNERS" insurance. If, by chance, you enter through the "LIFE INSURANCE" window first, you may want to offer them a "2nd Opinion" on both their "AUTO & HOMEOWNERS" Insurance Policies. The objective is to "clean out and clean up" each household. The other agents and carriers have got to go......because a "PROFESSIONAL INSURANCE CONSULTANT" has entered the building!!

If you are a LIFE & FINANCIAL SERVICES AGENT....... and do not have the multi-line advantage, set your "daily production goal" at a minimum of one sale per day. Consider the following:

ONE (1) $79 per month sale.....<u>EACH DAY</u>..... (which is equivalent to $948 in Annual Premiums).....for five (5) days....will generate <u>$4,740</u> of Life Production EACH WEEK. If you were to "average" $4,740 per week for 52 weeks, that level of production would generate $246,480 PER YEAR in LIFE SALES and a six-figure income....... As a result of your hard work and dedication to helping others to secure the "financial future" of THEIR FAMILIES. <u>LIFE</u> IS GOOD.......<u>LIFE</u> IS GREAT! It's an opportunity for you to "set yourself apart" and "show your professionalism" to your clients by YOUR ACTIONS.

Maximizing The "Geometric Progression" Referral System!

Have you ever considered building a **_Multi-Level_** Marketing...... <u>REFERRAL SYSTEM?"</u> For years, we "partnered" with our clients and prospects to create a "Geometric Progression....Multi-Level Marketing.... Referral System." Here's how it works:

- I started my agency with a <u>LIST</u> of 100 people that I knew and respected. It's important to work with people who respect <u>you</u> as well. If you already have a book of business.....hopefully, you've already built some "great" relationships....so just select 100 people from your book of business.

- I used a "<u>Pre-Approach</u> Direct Mail Package" prior to making contact with them....because some of them did not even know that I was in the insurance industry until they received the package.

- The "Pre-Approach" package was designed to "set the tone" for my follow-up phone call.

- All I asked of them was an "opportunity" to provide them with a 2nd opinion on their Auto-Home and/ or Life Policies. Since most of them "respected" <u>MY</u> opinion, most of them gave me that opportunity. During the time that I started my agency, in most cases, I knew that I could offer them a better "PRICE" than most of the other companies could......but my standard approach was "perhaps we can offer you a "BETTER VALUE."

- In the process of providing a 2nd opinion.........in many cases, I was able to "point out" and address some of the "loop-holes" in their current policies that their "AGENTS" had never discussed with them. Unfortunately, some clients have not seen their "so-called agent" in years......but, fortunately for you, that situation presents an OPPORTUNITY for YOU to become their agent.

- At any rate, some folks "switched" to my agency and some did not. No matter what THEY decided to do......... in addition to offering a 2nd opinion, MY MISSION was to provide them with a level of "service" that they had never experienced before. My goal was to become a "resource center"...... and an agency where they could get "information, education and a clear understanding" of the insurance products that they had been buying for years from other agents (who, apparently, did not think it was worth the time to explain the products and coverages).

- I also wanted to establish the fact that there was NO OBLIGATION ON THEIR PART to buy anything. My mission was to provide the information that they needed to make "intelligent and informed" decisions whether they did business with my agency or not. By taking this approach, we were able to build some very "trusting and lasting" relationships.

- If they decided to buy from our agency.......once we took care of "their business," I decided to "partner" with them to take care of "my business." Here's the word track that I used with EVERY ONE OF THEM (if you decide to use it, make it your own......talk like YOU talk and walk like YOU walk) :

"I want to, personally, THANK YOU for giving us the opportunity to SERVE YOU. One of our goals is to build our agency with GOOD QUALITY PEOPLE like you. Is there anybody else that you care about that you'd like me to share this with?"

The goal here is to obtain 3 referrals per contact. In most cases, if you've provided "great service, they will be more than glad to recommend others."

In the above examples, we're only talking about 7 "legs".....A, B, C, D, E, F,& G. Can you imagine starting this process with 100 "legs."

Who Do They Know?

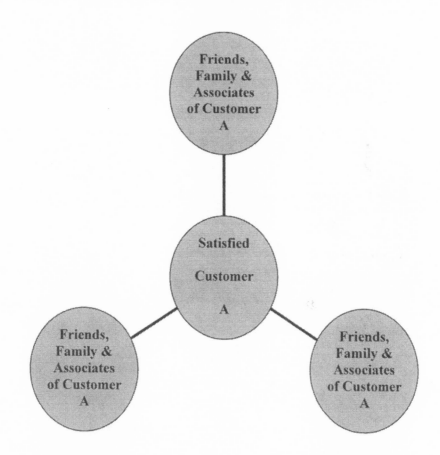

After obtaining the three (3) that you are going to contact, ask this question: "So would it be O.K. with you if I gave you three brochures to pass out to some of your other family members, friends and associates?"

If the answer was YES....I would give them a "personalized" Auto-Home (Tenant) and Life Insurance Brochure (with all of my contact information already pre-printed on the brochures). By having the opportunity to give them the three brochures, I was also cross selling some of my other lines to THEM "subliminally." And many times, I would receive telephone calls from people who had received those brochures. It became a great "partnership."

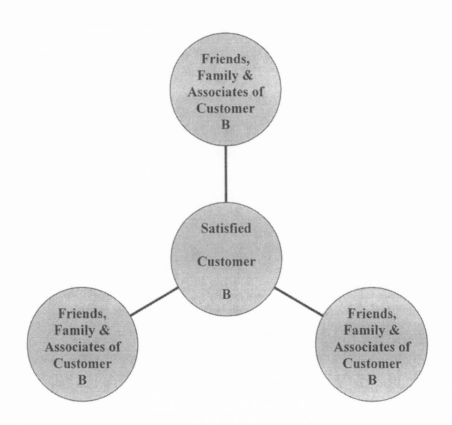

Let's Consider The Possibilities

- If you "partner" with each "satisfied" customer and <u>EARN</u> <u>THE RIGHT</u> to ask each one of them to recommend your agency and your services to three (3) family members, friends and/or associates..... <u>each one</u> of them could possibly deliver 3 new "prospects" to whom you can offer a 2nd opinion on their "Basic Three (Auto-Home-Life) Policies."

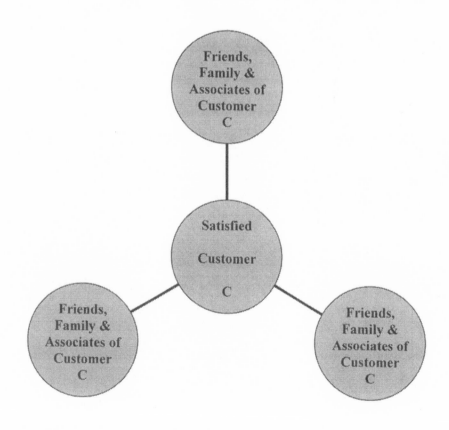

- So 100 "satisfied" customers may be able to deliver three hundred (300) "waiting to be satisfied" prospects to your agency............ to whom you can offer a 2nd opinion on their "Basic Three (Auto-Home-Life) Policies."

- And those 300 may be able to deliver 900 "waiting to be satisfied" prospects to your agency...to whom you can offer a 2nd opinion on their "Basic Three (Auto-Home-Life) Policies."

- And those 900 may be able to deliver 2,700 "waiting to be satisfied" prospects to your agency..... to whom you can offer a 2nd opinion on their "Basic Three (Auto-Home-Life) Policies."

Using this system......in the twenty two years that I had an agency........ I <u>ALWAYS</u> had a steady flow of people to talk to.....and I never had the time.....or the desire to spend money on elaborate yellow page advertisements and other "passive" forms of advertisement..... because when it's all said and done, you will discover that your best source of "quality" business will come from <u>REFERRALS</u>. It's very important that you install an "effective" referral system in your agency. So why not "partner" with your clients and prospects to create an <u>UNLIMITED</u> source of <u>REFERRALS.</u> They can lead you to people that you never would have had an opportunity to meet!

Here's a suggested word track for a PROSPECT who is not ready to buy from you <u>TODAY:</u>

"Thanks for giving us an opportunity to offer you a 2nd opinion on your insurance. One of our goals is to build our agency with GOOD QUALITY PEOPLE like you. So would it be O.K. with you if I gave you three brochures to pass out to your family, friends and associates? We'd like to offer them the same opportunity that we offered you: A Complimentary, No-Obligation, 2nd Opinion on their insurance needs."

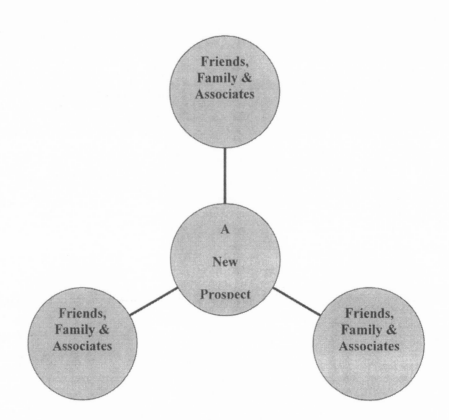

<u>Let's Review The Multi-Level</u>
<u>Marketing Referral System</u>

Level 1   The First 100 (Your Family, Friends & Associates)

Level 2   100 x 3 = 300 (Who Do THEY Know????)

Level 3   300 x 3 = 900 (And Who Do THEY Know???)

Level 4   900 x 3 = 2,700 (And Who Do THEY Know???)

This will put you in a position to market your products and services on "Multiple Levels"......and that's why I call it a "Multi-Level Marketing Referral System."

Which Level of Service Are You Providing?

Level 0 **"No-Human Connection Service"**
         (Offered Because You're Obligated To Do It)
Level 1 **"Ordinary" Service**
Level 2 **"Extra-Ordinary" Service**
Level 3 **"OUTSTANDING" Service**

Which "Level of Service" are you providing your clients and prospects? Which "Level of Service" do YOU expect from those with whom you do business? If YOU receive Level 0 or Level 1 service from a business, would YOU be excited about recommending that business to others? Absolutely NOT!!!

On the other hand.....if you receive "Extra-Ordinary" or "Outstanding" Service, would you be excited about recommending that business to others? YES YOU WOULD BE!!

I recently moved from one state to another and the service that I received from my new doctor was "OUTSTANDING!" So I asked <u>HIM</u> for some of his business cards to pass out to my family, friends and associates. He didn't have to ask me to recommend him. I asked HIM if I could recommend him. His NEXT CLIENT will be my wife!!!

Here's another case in point: The first "dry cleaner" that I used in Texas NEVER made the "Human Connection." So I found another dry cleaning service because, like most folks, I don't like being treated like a "number." At the NEW dry cleaning service......before I walk in the door to pick up my clothes..... they've already retrieved my clothes from the rack........ and have them ready for pick-up.....because they go into action when they see their customers "drive up." They know my vehicle, my name, my account number...and the way that I like my shirts and other clothes prepared. And when I walk in the door, they say "Mr. Pierre, your order is ready!" Now that's what I would call "OUTSTANDING SERVICE!" I've already recommended five new clients and four of the five have become steady customers.

When you go to a restaurant and receive GREAT FOOD and "OUTSTANDING SERVICE," are you excited about telling others about your experience? How many people will go to that restaurant based on YOUR RECOMMENDATION? And how many others will they recommend? And how many others will the others recommend?

The "Level of Service" that is being offered by your agency will determine your success in the Multi-Level Marketing Referral System. Offering "OUTSTANDING SERVICE" to your clients and prospects will pay huge dividends in the long run. The idea is to start with the "original" clients and prospects that YOU KNOW...and then to work each "referral" line as deep as you can with the prospects that THEY KNOW!! One day you may look back and find yourself marketing your products and services 6 to 10 levels deep from the original ones.

Everybody in your agency MUST UNDERSTAND the mission....... And the need to offer "OUTSTANDING SERVICE" to EVERY CLIENT AND EVERY PROSPECT at ALL TIMES!

"The Daily Power Sweep" Prospecting System

Daily Activity......Daily Activity......Daily Activity

STAY ON OFFENSE!!!!

Don't Wait For THEM To Contact YOU......

CONTACT THEM!!!

INTERACT WITH CLIENTS AND PROSPECTS

EVERY DAY!!!

What Can I Do **TODAY?**

<u>**MONDAY**</u> **(Day 1):**

- **Mail 5 Letters or Company-Produced Brochures On <u>EACH</u> of the following lines of business:**

    1. Auto Insurance   (5)
    2. Homeowners Insurance   (5)
    3. Life Insurance   (5)
    4. Commercial Insurance   (5)
    5. Flood Insurance   (5)
    6. Tenant Insurance   (5)

<u>**TUESDAY**</u> **(Day 2):**

- **Mail 5 Letters or Company-Produced Brochures On <u>EACH</u> of the following lines of business:**

    1. Auto Insurance   (5)
    2. Homeowners Insurance   (5)
    3. Life Insurance   (5)
    4. Commercial Insurance   (5)
    5. Flood Insurance   (5)
    6. Tenant Insurance   (5)

WEDNESDAY (Day 3):

- **Mail 5 Letters or Company-Produced Brochures On <u>EACH</u> of the following lines of business:**

1.	Auto Insurance	(5)
2.	Homeowners Insurance	(5)
3.	Life Insurance	(5)
4.	Commercial Insurance	(5)
5.	Flood Insurance	(5)
6.	Tenant Insurance	(5)

THURSDAY (Day 4):

- **Mail 5 Letters or Company-Produced Brochures On <u>EACH</u> of the following lines of business:**

1.	Auto Insurance	(5)
2.	Homeowners Insurance	(5)
3.	Life Insurance	(5)
4.	Commercial Insurance	(5)
5.	Flood Insurance	(5)
6.	Tenant Insurance	(5)

FRIDAY (Day 5):

- **MAIL** 5 Letters or Company-Produced Brochures On **EACH** of the following lines of business:

  1. Auto Insurance   (5)
  2. Homeowners Insurance   (5)
  3. Life Insurance   (5)
  4. Commercial Insurance   (5)
  5. Flood Insurance   (5)
  6. Tenant Insurance   (5)

- **CALL** the ones that you mailed the Letters/ Brochures to on last **MONDAY** to CROSS-SELL or to OFFER them a Complimentary- No Obligation-2nd Opinion:

  1. 5 Follow-Up Phone Calls about Auto Insurance
  2. 5 Follow-Up Phone Calls about Homeowners Insurance
  3. 5 Follow-Up Phone Calls about Life Insurance
  4. 5 Follow-Up Phone Calls about Commercial Insurance
  5. 5 Follow-Up Phone Calls about Flood Insurance
  6. 5 Follow-Up Phone Calls about Tenant Insurance

- **<u>CALL</u>** 5 of your upcoming RENEWALS from your current book of business........ 60 DAYS in advance...to review, update, upgrade or just to say THANK YOU FOR THE BUSINESS.

- **<u>MAKE</u>** THREE (3) SALES TODAY.

- **<u>OBTAIN</u>** a minimum of THREE (3) REFERRALS TODAY.

MONDAY (Day 6):

- **MAIL** 5 Letters or Company-Produced Brochures On **EACH** of the following lines of business:

  1. Auto Insurance   (5)
  2. Homeowners Insurance   (5)
  3. Life Insurance   (5)
  4. Commercial Insurance   (5)
  5. Flood Insurance   (5)
  6. Tenant Insurance   (5)

- **CALL** the ones that you mailed the Letters/ Brochures to on last **TUESDAY** to CROSS- SELL or to OFFER them a Complimentary- No Obligation-2nd Opinion:

  1. 5 Follow-Up Phone Calls about Auto Insurance
  2. 5 Follow-Up Phone Calls about Homeowners Insurance
  3. 5 Follow-Up Phone Calls about Life Insurance
  4. 5 Follow-Up Phone Calls about Commercial Insurance
  5. 5 Follow-Up Phone Calls about Flood Insurance
  6. 5 Follow-Up Phone Calls about Tenant Insurance

- **<u>CALL</u>** 5 of your upcoming RENEWALS from your current book of business........ 60 DAYS in advance...to review, update, upgrade or just to say THANK YOU FOR THE BUSINESS.

- **<u>MAKE</u>** THREE (3) SALES TODAY.

- **<u>OBTAIN</u>** a minimum of THREE (3) REFERRALS TODAY.

TUESDAY (Day 7):

- **MAIL** 5 Letters or Company-Produced Brochures On **EACH** of the following lines of business:

1.	Auto Insurance	(5)
2.	Homeowners Insurance	(5)
3.	Life Insurance	(5)
4.	Commercial Insurance	(5)
5.	Flood Insurance	(5)
6.	Tenant Insurance	(5)

- **CALL** the ones that you mailed the Letters/ Brochures to on last **WEDNESDAY** to CROSS-SELL or to OFFER them a Complimentary-No Obligation-2nd Opinion:

  1. 5 Follow-Up Phone Calls about Auto Insurance
  2. 5 Follow-Up Phone Calls about Homeowners Insurance
  3. 5 Follow-Up Phone Calls about Life Insurance
  4. 5 Follow-Up Phone Calls about Commercial Insurance
  5. 5 Follow-Up Phone Calls about Flood Insurance
  6. 5 Follow-Up Phone Calls about Tenant Insurance

- **<u>CALL</u>** 5 of your upcoming RENEWALS from your current book of business........ 60 DAYS in advance...to review, update, upgrade or just to say THANK YOU FOR THE BUSINESS.

- **<u>MAKE</u>** THREE (3) SALES TODAY.

- **<u>OBTAIN</u>** a minimum of THREE (3) REFERRALS TODAY.

WEDNESDAY (Day 8):

- **MAIL 5 Letters or Company-Produced Brochures On EACH of the following lines of business:**

  1. Auto Insurance   (5)
  2. Homeowners Insurance   (5)
  3. Life Insurance   (5)
  4. Commercial Insurance   (5)
  5. Flood Insurance   (5)
  6. Tenant Insurance   (5)

- **CALL the ones that you mailed the Letters/ Brochures to on last THURSDAY to CROSS-SELL or to OFFER them a Complimentary-No Obligation-2ⁿᵈ Opinion:**

  1. 5 Follow-Up Phone Calls about Auto Insurance
  2. 5 Follow-Up Phone Calls about Homeowners Insurance
  3. 5 Follow-Up Phone Calls about Life Insurance
  4. 5 Follow-Up Phone Calls about Commercial Insurance
  5. 5 Follow-Up Phone Calls about Flood Insurance
  6. 5 Follow-Up Phone Calls about Tenant Insurance

- **<u>CALL</u> 5 of your upcoming RENEWALS from your current book of business........ 60 DAYS in advance...to review, update, upgrade or just to say THANK YOU FOR THE BUSINESS.**

- **<u>MAKE</u> THREE (3) SALES TODAY.**

- **<u>OBTAIN</u> a minimum of THREE (3) REFERRALS TODAY.**

THURSDAY (Day 9):

- **MAIL** 5 Letters or Company-Produced Brochures On **EACH** of the following lines of business:

  1. Auto Insurance   (5)
  2. Homeowners Insurance   (5)
  3. Life Insurance   (5)
  4. Commercial Insurance   (5)
  5. Flood Insurance   (5)
  6. Tenant Insurance   (5)

- **CALL** the ones that you mailed the Letters/ Brochures to on last **FRIDAY** to CROSS-SELL or to OFFER them a Complimentary- No Obligation-2nd Opinion:

  1. 5 Follow-Up Phone Calls about Auto Insurance
  2. 5 Follow-Up Phone Calls about Homeowners Insurance
  3. 5 Follow-Up Phone Calls about Life Insurance
  4. 5 Follow-Up Phone Calls about Commercial Insurance
  5. 5 Follow-Up Phone Calls about Flood Insurance
  6. 5 Follow-Up Phone Calls about Tenant Insurance

- **<u>CALL</u>** 5 of your upcoming RENEWALS from your current book of business........ 60 DAYS in advance...to review, update, upgrade or just to say THANK YOU FOR THE BUSINESS.

- **<u>MAKE</u>** THREE (3) SALES TODAY.

- **<u>OBTAIN</u>** a minimum of THREE (3) REFERRALS TODAY.

FRIDAY (Day 10):

- **MAIL** 5 Letters or **Company-Produced Brochures On EACH** of the following lines of business:

  1. Auto Insurance (5)
  2. Homeowners Insurance (5)
  3. Life Insurance (5)
  4. Commercial Insurance (5)
  5. Flood Insurance (5)
  6. Tenant Insurance (5)

- **CALL** the ones that you mailed the Letters/ Brochures to on last **MONDAY** to CROSS-SELL or to OFFER them a Complimentary- No Obligation-2nd Opinion:

  1. 5 Follow-Up Phone Calls about Auto Insurance
  2. 5 Follow-Up Phone Calls about Homeowners Insurance
  3. 5 Follow-Up Phone Calls about Life Insurance
  4. 5 Follow-Up Phone Calls about Commercial Insurance
  5. 5 Follow-Up Phone Calls about Flood Insurance
  6. 5 Follow-Up Phone Calls about Tenant Insurance

- **<u>CALL</u>** 5 of your upcoming RENEWALS from your current book of business........ 60 DAYS in advance...to review, update, upgrade or just to say THANK YOU FOR THE BUSINESS.

- **<u>MAKE</u>** THREE (3) SALES TODAY.

- **<u>OBTAIN</u>** a minimum of THREE (3) REFERRALS TODAY.

Summary of The Activity For The Week

- **30 Letters/Brochures Mailed <u>Each Day</u> To Advertise Your Agency, Products and Services**
  = 150 Weekly

- **30 Follow-Up Phone Calls Made <u>Each Day</u> To Cross Sell or To Offer A 2nd Opinion**
  = 150 Weekly

- **3 New Sales <u>Each Day</u>**
  = 15 Weekly

- **3 Referrals Obtained <u>Each Day</u>**
  = 15 Weekly

- **5 Renewal Calls Made <u>Each Day</u>**
  = 25 Weekly

Key Points:

- In 30 years, I've NEVER made a telephone call WITHOUT SENDING MY <u>MESSAGE</u> and MY <u>MESSENGERS</u> FIRST!!

- My MESSENGERS are the COMPANY-PRODUCED BROCHURES and the COMPANY-PRODUCED DIRECT MAIL LETTERS.

- By the time I make the follow-up phone call, I can determine their level of interest by <u>LISTENING</u> very carefully to their responses, reactions and the tone in their voices.

- If they agree to an appointment, that "signifies" an interest in the product or service that I'm offering. So we'll start the process on the 50 yard line and a "touchdown" is already in "sight."

- When I get together for the actual appointment, I let <u>THEM TALK</u> while I <u>LISTEN</u>.....because my MESSENGER has already delivered the "highlights" of my message. I discovered many years ago that you can learn more by letting others talk....while YOU LISTEN......because you already know what YOU know.....but you won't ever know what THEY KNOW.....unless you let THEM TALK.

- However, my goal is to "meet them where THEY ARE" and to explain the coverages and the options in language that THEY understand. Once we address any concerns that they have, we CLOSE THE SALE. After we close the sale and have secured the required paperwork and payment, we OBTAIN REFERRALS.

- On the other hand......if they are rude or unresponsive when you make the follow-up phone call, that's a sign that they MAY NOT HAVE AN INTEREST in what you have to offer TODAY. Thank them for the opportunity to speak with them and exit gracefully. When you mailed the letter or brochure, you offered them an opportunity to transfer that risk from their family to the insurance company....and, if they reject it.....they can never say that you did not make that offer!

- So don't get hung up on it one way or the other. If they are INTERESTED.....set an appointment..... explain the coverages options and payment plans in plain easy-to-understand language.....address their concerns....<u>Close the Sale</u> and <u>Obtain Referrals.</u> If they are NOT interested, please don't take it personally...just move on to the next one. Some Will...Some Won't....So What! Do what YOU do.....Control what YOU can control (YOUR Actions and YOUR Activities)!

I call it the "DAILY POWER SWEEP" because each day you will do the following:

- **Send out "Agent Level Marketing Materials" for NEW Auto-Home-Life-Commercial-Flood- and Tenant Insurance Business.**
- **Make Follow-Up phone calls to Cross-Sell or offer 2nd Opinions on Auto-Home-Life-Commercial-Flood and Tenant Insurance.**
- **Interact with 5 of your Renewal Clients.**
- **Position yourself to make 3 Sales Per Day.**
- **Position yourself to obtain a minimum of 3 Referrals Per Day.**

**New Business.....New Sales.....Renewals......
Referrals.
Now That's What I Call A SWEEP!!!**

Will this system work out perfectly EVERY day....and EVERY week? NO!

Will your sales increase? With all of the <u>INCREASED ACTIVITY</u>, I would say YES.....because now...you have installed a "Daily" Roadmap to Success! What do you have to lose by TRYING IT?

What would happen to your activity and your sales if you had two or more associates in your agency who were able to DUPLICATE THIS PATTERN? Would you ever run out of people to talk to? Think about the possibilities!

Remember The Golden Rule

<u>The "Golden Rule" Rules!!!</u> Always remember to "do unto others as you would have them do unto you." Treat clients and prospects like you would want to be treated. Whatever you do, make sure that the client/prospect will benefit <u>more than you do</u>.....and that the transaction will be "in favor of" the client/prospect.

Remember The "MOMMA" Rule

If it's not good enough to sell to your MOMMA......it's not good enough to sell to a client or a prospect!!!

MP

NOTES:

_____
_____
_____
_____
_____
_____
_____
_____

My Action Plan

_____
_____
_____
_____
_____
_____
_____
_____
_____
_____
_____

<u>Where Do You Want To Be</u>
<u>36 Months From NOW?</u>

	<u>Now</u>	<u>36 Months From Now</u>
Total P & C Sales Per Year	_____	_____
Total P & C Commissions	_____	_____
Total Policies In Force	_____	_____
Total Life Sales Per Year	_____	_____
Commissions-Life Sales	_____	_____
Multi-Line Percentage	_____	_____
Loss Ratio	_____	_____
Retention	_____	_____
Referrals Per Year	_____	_____

So How Do You Build:

A $1,000,000 Per Year Agency?
A $2,000,000 Per Year Agency?
A $5,000,000 Per Year Agency?
A $10,000,000 Per Year Agency?

ONE DAY AT A TIME!

In Closing

For every <u>action</u>......there's a <u>reaction</u>. Sometimes we can control the REACTION, in advance......based on the ACTION that we take or fail to take. For example, when we bought our first home in 1977, the "agent" must have <u>assumed</u> that I knew what a "Dec Page" was and that I could explain the coverages on a Homeowners Policy to MYSELF. I could not!!! I've had courses in Algebra, Physics, Calculus, Foreign Languages, Geometry, Trigonometry, and many others....but, up to that point, had never had a course in INSURANCE, INSURANCE COVERAGES, AUTO, HOMEOWNERS OR OTHER INSURANCE CONTRACTS. How many of YOUR CLIENTS have had a course in Insurance? That's why they need YOU to "Explain and Educate" them on Auto, Home, Life, Flood, Commercial, Personal Umbrella Policies, etc. A quote is a quote.....and that's all that it is! But what's behind the numbers?

It's not the job of the client to build a relationship with the agent. On the contrary, it's the job of the AGENT to build a relationship with the client. How could my first homeowners "agent" expect to RETAIN me as a client when he simply "took my order" for a Homeowners Policy.........gave me a QUOTE.........and wrote the application. He never explained the coverages......nor did he ever say "THANK YOU".......nor did he ever make contact with me again. His ACTIONS (or lack thereof) caused me to SHOP with a determination to SWITCH to a more <u>PROFESSIONAL INSURANCE CONSULTANT.</u> I didn't need an "agent." I needed a "consultant!" There's a big difference between an "agent" and a "Professional Consultant."

I said all of that to say this:

- Do you have pro-active processes in place to RETAIN YOUR CLIENTS? I would ask you to review the contact files for 25 to 50 of your clients (as a sample) to determine if each of those clients have been contacted, at least, once per year.

- Do you have "relationship-building" processes in place to let your clients know that you <u>REALLY</u> "value" them as a client? My first homeowners "agent" made no effort to build a relationship. Therefore, I severed the ties to that agent and that agency! Have you lost any clients like that?

- How could an "agent" expect the RETENTION to be "HIGH" if there are no processes in place to "touch" clients on a regular basis (like every six months or every twelve months)?

- Competition for market share is more intense today than ever before.......so why would (or should) a client remain LOYAL to an agent who is not LOYAL to them?

- <u>NOW IS A GOOD TIME</u>.....to make an appointment with each and every one of your clients and review their Auto, Home, Life and Flood Policies. You will find UNLIMITED OPPORTUNITIES to write NEW BUSINESS right there in your own book of business!

- Who's running YOUR agency? An "Office Manager," the CSR or the CEO? When is the last time <u>YOU</u> had an opportunity to "interact" with YOUR OWN CLIENTS?

- Keep a <u>genuine smile</u> in your heart.....so that it will show on your face.....and give notice to all who comes in contact with you.....that YOU ARE WELCOME HERE....in this PLACE.... and in this SPACE!!!

*<u>That's All For Now Partners.....
But Before You Go...I Want To Share One
Last Thing.....</u>*

Every letter that came out of The Pierre Agency ended with a <u>"Thank You"</u> and an emphasis on "the OPPORTUNITY TO SERVE."

*<u>Writing This Book Has Been An OPPORTUNITY To Serve
YOU, The Agent</u>*

So......<u>THANKS</u> for the <u>OPPORTUNITY</u> to serve <u>YOU</u>!

With All Good Wishes,

Melvin Pierre, Sr.
E-mail Address: melvin.pierre@yahoo.com